brilliant

parent

What the best parents know, do and say

Emma Sargent

PEARSON
Prentice Hall

Harlow, England • London • New York • Boston • San Francisco • Toronto • Sydney • Singapore • Hong Kong
Tokyo • Seoul • Taipei • New Delhi • Cape Town • Madrid • Mexico City • Amsterdam • Munich • Paris • Milan

PEARSON EDUCATION LIMITED

Edinburgh Gate
Harlow CM20 2JE
Tel: +44 (0)1279 623623
Fax: +44 (0)1279 431059
Website: www.pearsoned.co.uk

First published in Great Britain in 2009

ISBN: 978–0–273–72493–3

British Li
A catalog   :ary

Library o
Sargent,
  Brilliaı   na Sargent.
    p. cı
  ISBN
  1. Parε
  HQ75
  649'.1–

WORCESTERSHIRE
COUNTY COUNCIL

785	
Bertrams	16/07/2009
649.1	£9.99
DR	

10 9 8 7 6 5 4 3 2 1
13 12 11 10 09

Typeset in 10/14pt Plantin by 3
Printed and bound by Henry Ling Ltd, at the Dorset Press, Dorchester, Dorset

The publisher's policy is to use paper manufactured from sustainable forests.

Contents

Acknowledgements

Big thanks go to:

Rachael Stock, publisher, who not only agreed to take on this project but managed it and me so marvellously.

Charlie Warburton, who introduced me to Rachael.

Friends, old and new, who support me and who were so positive about my first book, *Flying Start*.

Everyone who contributed their stories. My apologies to those who provided me with stories that I wasn't able to fit in. Some names have been changed.

Everyone who has made encouraging comments and been enthusiastic about this project. Every single comment has contributed to my motivation.

And most of all my family, Tim, Thomas and Hannah.

About the author

Emma balances being a parent of two with running a coaching and speaking business. She has a reputation as an extremely knowledgeable, effective and inspirational speaker and works all over the world. She has a psychology degree and is a certified trainer of NLP. People particularly enjoy her no-nonsense, yet warm, approach to personal development; she cuts through the fluff to give practical 'how to' solutions. She is less concerned with theory and more with what works. Her passion is the future of our children and what we, their parents, can do on a day to day basis to help them have the best chance in life.

You will find even more ways to help your children help themselves, and build great relationships with them, on her blog www.BrilliantParent.com

Introduction

For me, being a parent is the most challenging job I've ever had – at times wonderful, fun and joyous, at other times frustrating, monotonous and exhausting. It's also something for which I am extremely grateful. I have learned a great deal from my children in their young lives, including a lot about myself, some of which I would have preferred not to have learned!

My experience, and also that of my friends, is that our children seem to have been put on this earth specifically to test us in every way possible, to press every button and to provide us with an emotional rollercoaster to ride on a daily basis! This can leave us feeling frustrated and tired, and as if parenthood is a thankless task.

On the other hand, we also have times when everything is going well, when we feel great, our children are really engaged with us and we feel we might burst with love and pride.

And then there are our hopes and fears. Are our children going to turn out all right? Will they make the most of their lives? Will they be happy? Many of us worry about how much of this is down to our parenting.

The fact is that we can only do our best; we are not perfect. I like to think that we are all 'work in progress' and as long as we are constantly learning, asking ourselves questions and striving to be our best then that's what's important. Sometimes we manage to do a great job, sometimes we don't. Sometimes we will get it right, sometimes we won't.

Being a brilliant parent is not about being perfect. It's about going above and beyond the things that make us good parents: love, support and nurturing. This is about thinking a bit bigger and at a different level, beyond basic care. It's about getting to know how your children think and how you can best handle their behaviour – and your own. It's about the things you can teach them without them realising what you're doing – things like thinking for themselves, developing personal responsibility, being self-aware and aware of others, and generally helping them to make the most of what they have, and ultimately helping them to live their best lives.

Being a brilliant parent involves a level of understanding of your children that will help you to help them in ways that you may never even have thought possible.

I recently met a woman called Lindsay. She has a 17-year-old daughter, Corinne. When she was about 13, Corinne started retching and sometimes being physically sick before school. It happened, on average, on three out of the five school days per week. This went on for *four* years, during which time she stopped eating breakfast altogether in an attempt to stop the sickness. Imagine what that must have done for her concentration at that important time in her life.

Lindsay was driving Corinne to college just a couple of months ago when Corinne asked her to stop the car so that she could be sick. When she got back into the car, Lindsay said, 'Corinne, this has got to stop'. 'Mum', she replied, 'I know. There's a counsellor at college and I'm going to go and see them.' It only took a couple of sessions for the counsellor to find out that Corinne was making herself sick with anxiety about having the *right books for the day's lessons.* How did it start? It all started when her teacher bellowed at her in front of the class just once too often for not having the right books for the day.

When I remarked that it was amazing that Corinne had kept it up for four whole years, through changes of teachers and even changing schools, Lindsay agreed. She said that she was a bit hurt that she hadn't been able to help her daughter. She said to me, 'Nothing I said to her made any difference.'

I pointed out to her that usually it's not what we *say* that makes a difference, it's what we *ask*. Lindsay looked at me as if I had hit her over the head with a spade. 'Oh my God, you're right. I didn't know how to find out.'

> it's not what we *say* that makes a difference, it's what we *ask*

In this book, I will show you how to think and ask questions in ways that mean you *will* know how to find out what is going on in the mind of your child and be better able to help them to help themselves.

I will also share simple strategies and show you how to teach your children to think in a way that will help them to overcome everyday obstacles such as not wanting to do homework, arguing with friends, or worrying about something like exams.

This book will also help them to know and get more of what they want out of life. Most people are adults before they become really aware of what's important to them, what motivates them, how they create their successes and how they limit themselves. Wouldn't it be great for all children to have the benefit of that knowledge so much earlier?

Here's an example of the empowering nature of self-awareness, even when you are seven years old. My son Thomas used to get frustrated very easily if he didn't understand something straight away. On this particular day, he was having a go at a fairly simple logic problem when he got stuck. It was one of those 'have a go at this everyone' problems you glibly chuck at the family, which you think is going to be fun, and then you wish you hadn't! As soon as he got stuck, I saw his frustration appear, which meant that it was game over as far as his ability to think clearly and creatively was concerned. The rest of the family tried to explain it to him, but of course he wasn't in the mood to hear or understand anything. I said to him gently, 'When I'm frustrated and can't understand something, it's like a dark grey fog comes down in front of my eyes, and I know that it is hard for me to carry on thinking. What happens to you?'

Thomas: *My fog's not grey, it's red.*

Me: *So it's red.*

I used a very interested tone, partly because I was genuinely interested and partly because I really wanted to encourage him to tell me more. Repeating his words also helps because he feels heard.

Thomas: *Yes. And it's like a curtain that closes.*

Me: *Wow. So, when I understand and can think clearly, it's bright in my head, sort of white. What's yours?*

Thomas: *It's bright green. And actually there are lights, too. When I start to understand, I can see a green light through the red curtain.*

Bear with me reader! I know this sounds completely bizarre.

Thomas now has an awareness of understanding versus not understanding. Understanding is green and not understanding is red. This awareness, on its own, has meant that 'not understanding' does not lead to such a high level of frustration any more. Even three years after this initial conversation, if he doesn't understand something, when I try to explain, he will say

'Oh yes, it's a sort of orangey green now' and both of us know that he is on his way to understanding.

Being a brilliant parent means being able to raise your child's self-awareness to increase the level of choice that they have in the way they interact with others and live their lives as successfully as they want to.

If we want to be brilliant parents we also need to spend some time becoming aware of our own successes and shortcomings so that we can truly give the best of ourselves in the precious years that we spend with our children, helping to shape their future.

So, although this book is primarily for your children, it is also for you.

CHAPTER 1

What is a brilliant parent?

Being a brilliant parent doesn't mean being a perfect parent. We are human. That means that we are all different, that we all handle things in different ways and that, yes, we make mistakes. There are lots of right ways to be a brilliant parent.

You are already well on the way to being a brilliant parent if you want to do your best for your children; if you are open to learning from other parents; if you are open to learning from your children. Most importantly you are becoming a brilliant parent if you already learn from yourself – from your own behaviour and the responses that you get from others. If you've ever kicked yourself for handling a situation in the wrong way and resolved to do better next time, you're already on the right track.

What brilliant parents know, do and say

You will recognise here some things you already do and other things that you may need to think about, change or improve.

In the following chapters I will expand on all the key qualities and abilities and give you proven and effective ways for you to incorporate them into your parenting. This means that you can easily learn the things that brilliant parents know, do and say.

What brilliant parents *know*

Brilliant parents know:

- what kind of a parent they are striving to be;
- what's important to them;
- what they will accept and what they won't accept from their children;
- that they are role models for their children, whether they like it or not;
- that we are all different and their children are not 'mini-me's'.

Let's take a look at each of these in turn:

Brilliant parents have a strong vision of the kind of parent they want to be

We all have an idea of what makes a great parent. You may base your parenting style on that of your own parents; you may do the exact opposite. You may have noticed other people's parents when you were growing up and thought 'I want to be like that when I have children'. Most likely, it will be a mixture of all these things.

Brilliant parents know what they are aiming for and work towards it.

Whatever your vision of a brilliant parent is, you may like to start to flesh it out now.

Brilliant parents know what's important to them

In other words, they have a set of strong, non-negotiable values around parenting.

What are values? They are the unconscious, unwritten rules that guide our lives. They underpin all our behaviour and inform what we think is right and wrong. We don't very often think about them, but it is incredibly useful to know what they are because then we can be more aware of whether or not we are living up to them. 'Do as I say, not as I do' is an example of *not* living your values!

Brilliant parents are very clear about what they will and will not accept

Our behaviour is driven by, and is a true reflection of, our values. It was fashionable not too long ago to let your child be a free spirit and find their own boundaries. We now know that approach can create many problems for children. Having strong boundaries in place at home allows children to test them and know their place in their world.

It is very likely that it is in this area that you will encounter conflict with your children. You need to be prepared to explain to them why you won't let them do things that other children are allowed to do or vice versa.

Brilliant parents know that they are role models for their children

This does not mean that you have to be perfect, but it is important to know that your children are learning from you, your partner and any other significant adult in their life when they are young. So you need to behave in line with your values and *be consistent*.

Brilliant parents also know that everyone is different

We all think differently and communicate differently. So brilliant parents make every effort to understand and get to know their children. Understanding how your child thinks and creates their own internal world is one of the main pieces of the jigsaw that makes a brilliant parent.

Our children are not mini versions of us. And however much we look for parts of ourselves in our children, we open up a whole new world when we begin instead to notice how they are different and celebrate this fact. It's so important to allow our children to be themselves and live their dreams, not ours.

What brilliant parents *do*

Brilliant parents:

- think about outcomes before providing solutions;
- notice everything;
- listen brilliantly;
- behave in line with their values;
- show consistency in the way they treat their children and each other;
- manage their emotions effectively.

Brilliant parents have an effective way of thinking about situations

Brilliant parents make use of a Brilliant Framework, or way of thinking about situations, which is best explained in the diagram below.

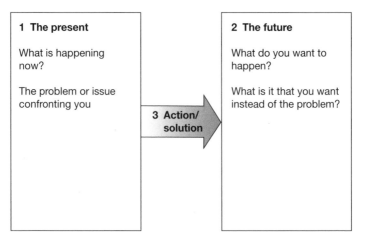

1 The present

What is happening now?

The problem or issue confronting you

3 Action/ solution

2 The future

What do you want to happen?

What is it that you want instead of the problem?

It's a very simple, yet amazingly powerful way of thinking.

The sequence of **present–future–action** may seem obvious. It makes sense, doesn't it, to think about what the situation is now, what we want instead, and then decide on what action to take? What is extraordinary is how seldom we actually do it this way.

For example, have you ever had a problem and discussed it with a friend? You tell them a bit about your problem and they start to offer you solutions because they care about you and don't want you to have the problem any more. They are focusing on ways to get you *out of your problem*.

You think about the solutions as they suggest them, but none of them seems to quite fit. Then you hear yourself explaining why the solutions wouldn't work or agreeing in a half-hearted way that you could try them because you don't want to offend your friend.

Why do you do this? Because you may not be sure about what you want.

When we have a problem, we find it difficult to focus on what we want, instead of on the problem. We know that we don't want the problem but we don't know what we want to happen instead.

> we find it difficult to focus on what we want, instead of on the problem

The most useful thing that anybody can do when you have a problem is to help you to work out what you really want. Once you know that, it is quite likely that you will know what action to take yourself.

This is in essence a simple process, and it is its simplicity that makes it easy to use once you get the hang of it.

Once you get used to thinking in this way and teaching your children to think like this, you will have taught them a skill that will help them to achieve more success in their lives.

Brilliant parents notice everything

This is the 'eyes in the back of the head' skill that some parents are well-known for!

One of the most important skills of a brilliant parent is in helping their children become self-aware; to know what they are good at, what impact their behaviour has on others, what talents they have, what makes them who they are.

To make someone aware of what they are doing, you need to be able to notice it first. You need to be good at noticing how someone is doing something, and really listening to what they are saying and what they are not saying.

Have you ever asked someone who is terrifically good at something, 'How do you do that?', only to be met with the reply, 'I don't know, I just do it'? That is because they are naturally good, and have never had to consciously think it through.

So it is with our children. When we get really good at noticing small things in our child's behaviour, we can help them become aware of how they do things well; how they think; how they may be creating their own problems; how they learn; and how they can make the most of their qualities. It is very exciting to be able to help a child unlock some of their unconscious processes to propel them towards success, so Chapter 4 will help you to unlock the secrets of your child's inner world.

Brilliant parents listen brilliantly

We also need to be able to really listen – not only to what someone is saying, but *how* they are saying it. Imagine how useful it would be to be able to notice when your child is using language that limits them. And not only to notice this, but to be able to help them become aware of their internal thinking processes that may be preventing them from getting what they want. If you want to be a brilliant listener then Chapter 5 is for you!

Brilliant parents behave in line with their values

If *honesty* is really important to you, be honest with your children. (Though remember there are times when being fully and completely honest is not the best policy.)

If *persistence* is a quality that is important to you, demonstrate persistence when you want to achieve something.

If *standing up for yourself* is something you want your children to learn, make sure that you can stand up for yourself, too.

If you don't like *dealing with conflict* in day-to-day events, for example, how will you teach your children the importance of facing conflict and dealing with it in a positive way?

It is not always easy living up to your own values.

Brilliant parents are consistent in their behaviour

This means being consistent with their children and with each other (if they have a partner). It sounds so simple, but practically everybody I know struggles to be consistent.

Just last week I banned my son from watching a particular television programme as a punishment for being rude, and he clearly didn't believe that I was going to go through with it. After all, I wanted to watch the programme too.

I said to my daughter, 'He doesn't believe me does he?' She replied, 'No offence Mummy, but you do sometimes give in.' And of course, she was right, I do sometimes give in. I give in because I want them to have a lovely time and I love them, blah, blah, blah . . . But it's not OK to threaten something and not go through with it. Even sometimes. Why? Because, as became clear here, your children won't believe you and you lose their respect.

Brilliant parents manage their emotions effectively

I have devoted the whole of Chapter 3 to managing emotions. It contains some really effective strategies for emotional management that are proven to work.

What brilliant parents *say*

Brilliant parents:

● communicate effectively;

● give feedback that is honest, realistic and kind;

● use language positively to build confidence and get results;

● ask questions more often than they give advice.

Brilliant parents are great communicators

Brilliant parents understand that communication is the foundation of all that we do and, through what they say and ask, they teach their children to be great communicators.

Brilliant parents give great feedback

Our children need to have feedback on their behaviour that is honest and realistic. If we give them feedback on their behaviour, it makes them aware; and awareness gives them choices. They do not have a choice of changing if they are not aware of their behaviour.

We are not helping our children if we tell them that everything they do is brilliant. Feedback from other people in their lives will not always be that positive and they need to feel secure in their own opinions of themselves. There is a fine line between self-confidence and self-delusion.

We want our children to be happy and confident in their lives, to grow their true talents and be themselves. So we need to give them feedback that enables them to capitalise on their strengths and offers them the chance to change the things that are not working for them.

Brilliant parents use language that builds self-esteem and gets results

When brilliant parents talk to their children:

- they think of the effect or consequence of the message;
- they think of what they want to happen as a result of what they are saying;
- they think about what impact their words will have in the minds of their children and on their children's behaviour.

Chapter 6 is full of examples and strategies that will enable you to use language powerfully and naturally to help your child's development.

Brilliant parents ask brilliant questions

The ability to ask good questions is an incredibly powerful skill. It is crucial if you want to really understand your child and how they think.

I wish that I had been taught how to ask questions at school, rather than leave it to luck. Sometimes just one question, carefully chosen, can make a problem disappear.

Questions can be the key to helping someone to think through a problem, think through what they want and help them achieve their outcome.

> questions can be the key to helping someone to think through a problem

Help children to learn how to question, and you teach them to be interested, to form their own opinions and to learn effectively.

There really is no end to the benefits of being able to ask questions so in Chapter 5 I will give you the frameworks and skills you need to become a brilliant questioner.

CHAPTER 2

Starting with you

I f you want to be a brilliant parent, you first need to be aware of your own strengths and weaknesses. It's an important step in understanding the impact you may have on others. Remember, being a brilliant parent does not mean being perfect. It means being prepared to be honest with yourself and to put in the effort to be the best mum or dad you can be.

You also need to have a very clear vision of the parent you want to be and the values you want your children to have as adults. You are your child's most powerful role model from the moment they are born. Children are such incredible sponges when it comes to learning. They learn through imitation. We wonder sometimes where on earth our children's character traits come from, only to be met with raised eyebrows and amused grins from our partners and friends!

How often has one of your children said something that may have surprised you, only for you to realise it was a direct quote from you? I heard a great story recently of a little boy (now a grown man of 50!) who, aged five, had to go into hospital to have his tonsils out. He was in a hospital run by nuns who were extremely caring and gentle. Imagine their surprise when his answer to 'What would you like to drink?' was, 'I think I'll have a small sherry'! Straight from the mouth of his mother!

There is enough evidence around to indicate that what happens at home has an enormous impact on a child's development. Our

what happens at home has an enormous impact on a child's development

children are not just learning how to do things at home, they are learning ways of being in the world. They are forming their opinions, working out what's important to us and them, how to fit into society, how to interact with friends, what being part of a family means and so on. We must be aware of the messages they are getting from us, both spoken and unspoken, and the beliefs about themselves and the world around them that they are forming as a result.

Take, as an example, parents who talk about their children negatively within their earshot, as if the child is not going to be affected unless they are talking directly to them. I'm sure most people have heard a conversation that goes like this:

Debra: *Isn't Emily gorgeous?*

Emily's mother: *She looks it, doesn't she? But I can tell you at home she's revolting. Not like her brother at this age – he was an angel.*

What messages does Emily get about herself, her mother, her brother and her relationship to both of them? If Emily gets this message enough times – and at certain times in a young life, once is enough – she will start to fit into the role assigned to her by her mother and keep proving her mother right.

? brilliant questions

Remember the important part that each parent plays as a longer-term role model for their children. Ask yourself:

- What type of partner are your children going to look for as adults?
- What are they learning about relationships from you?
- Are they learning to respect each other or are they learning that it's OK to criticise each other?

- What is your son learning from his father; what is your daughter learning from her mother?
- What is your daughter learning from her father; what is your son learning from his mother?

Our enormous emotional investment in our children sometimes gets in the way of us being good role models. It seems so unfair that my children behave impeccably for other people and squabble and bicker with me. Even though I know that it is the same in every household (as far as I know), it frustrates and upsets me – why should the person who loves them and invests so much in them get the worst of their behaviour? I find it quite difficult in these moments to stay calm and, frankly, grown-up. I am well aware that they are testing boundaries with me because they know that they are safe to do so, but in that moment I just don't like it.

Day-to-day stuff gets in the way, too. We may be very busy with work or tired, and therefore short-tempered. We may be worried about something and the children think we are worried about them. Children do not respond well to anxiety from a parent; it makes them feel very wobbly indeed.

One of the things that stop us from being a consistently good role model is our ability to manage our state. If we get frustrated or angry, we are likely to behave in a way that is not useful either for us or our children. The next chapter is devoted to managing our emotions.

We need to strive for consistency, even though it can sometimes feel like an uphill battle. Children need consistency in their lives to feel safe and emotionally secure. The world is a scary enough place without us adding to it at home.

> children need consistency in their lives to feel safe and emotionally secure

The starting point is to become aware of what we are currently like as parents, good and bad; then to decide how we want to be as parents and equip ourselves to keep focused on that and maintain it.

You today – becoming aware

Remember the Brilliant Framework (page 6)?

The best place to start is always to think about the way things are now. You need to know what you do now so that you can do more of what you like and less of what you don't like. Self-awareness really is the critical first step to being a better parent. We all have a sense of what we do and say, but we rarely take time out to think about it and how it may affect the future of our children.

A friend of mine is usually in a hurry because she is usually late. She runs everywhere, with her children running behind her attempting to keep up while she shouts: 'Hurry up, hurry up, we're late again!' It wasn't until we had a conversation about how children are affected by our behaviour that she even realised that it was something she did almost all the time. Nor had she considered what negative messages her two children may be getting.

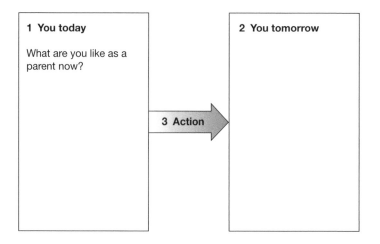

🡕 brilliant exercise

You today

Take a few moments to think about yourself. Here are some questions to guide your thinking. Jot the answers down so that we can revisit some of them later.

1 What's important to you in your life? What's important to you about being a parent?

2 What behaviour do you see in your children that you realise they have learned directly from you, both positive and negative?

3 What are you good at and find easy? (Be prepared – I asked my four-year-old daughter what I was good at and, after much deliberation, her answer was, 'Being cross.' That was feedback for me.)

4 What are you less good at and find less easy?

5 What qualities do you have that you hope to pass on to your children?

6 What characteristics do you have that you would prefer not to pass on to your children?

7 What are you enthusiastic or passionate about?

8 If you are a working parent, how do you balance work and home?

9 What do you like about being a parent?

10 What do you dislike?

11 What do you do that you want to stop doing or do less of?

12 What do you do that you want to do more of?

Perhaps some of those questions were ones that you had not considered before. What did you learn about yourself?

Ask your partner, if you have one, to answer these questions too. It is a great way to notice consistencies and inconsistencies

between you and to start a discussion about the areas you want
to change together.

Now let's move to what we want – 'you tomorrow'.

You tomorrow – how do you get what you want?

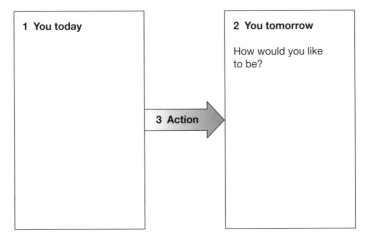

People who get what they want consistently in their lives all have
a similar strategy:

- They think about what they *do* want, not what they *don't*
  want.

- They mentally rehearse having it already.

- They think about the consequences of getting it, positive
  and negative, to themselves and those around them.

- They make sure that they can take action themselves,
  and that someone else is not responsible for the
  action.

Let's take those in turn.

Thinking about what you *do* want, not what you *don't* want

Our minds can't imagine 'not'. 'Not' only occurs in language, not in our thoughts. So if we tell ourselves not to do something, we are in fact instructing our mind to think of the very thing that we don't want.

Think for a minute about the following statements:

● I mustn't eat cake today.

● I don't want to lose my temper with my children.

● I must be careful not to slip.

As you read these statements, what images come to mind? Eating cake, having an argument and slipping over, probably! Whatever you imagine happening acts as an instruction to your unconscious mind to do it. We can't not think about what we don't want to think about until we have thought about it first!

It is much more effective to give yourself the following instructions as alternatives to the above statements:

● I will eat healthy food today.

● I will be calm and positive with my children today.

● I will walk carefully.

With these statements, you will imagine what you *do* want, rather than what you don't want.

Take a moment to think about whether you think about what you do want to happen or what you don't want to happen. It makes a big difference.

Mentally rehearsing having it already

We discovered that a friend's child has an effective strategy for running races. He imagines himself running across the winning line *having already won the race*. In other words, he mentally rehearses getting what he wants. The more sensory rich your rehearsal, the more likely it is that you will achieve your outcome.

Ask yourself, how would I know if I had achieved the outcome?
What would I see, hear and feel?

The boxer Muhammad Ali was excellent at mental rehearsal. He imagined he was in the future fighting his next opponent and went through the whole fight in his mind again and again. He coined the phrase 'creating future history' to describe this process.

Thinking about the consequences of getting it, both positive and negative

In other words, does what you want fit with who you are and what's important to you? Put yourself even further into the future and ask yourself: 'What will happen if I get what I want? Will I lose anything that I have now? How will it impact on those around me and is it worth it?'

These consequences play a huge role in our motivation to reach our goal. If the consequences are not compelling for us, we don't feel motivated to take action. If we actively think through all the consequences, in this case of becoming a brilliant parent, we will be highly motivated to take action and make the changes we need to.

The consequences of becoming a brilliant parent are far reaching – lasting way beyond your lifetime.

Making sure that you can take action yourself

We are only responsible for our own behaviour. We can't set an outcome for someone else to behave in a certain way and expect it to happen.

We have to look to ourselves first. What can *we* do differently that will make it more likely that the other person will behave differently towards us?

There are many parents who want their children to achieve specific things and a lot of their energy goes into their own personal outcomes for their children. They expect their children to go to university, be a doctor, lawyer, accountant, etc. My mother used to tell everyone I was going to be an accountant, which was the source of much annoyance to me. Once upon a time I was quite good at maths and this morphed over the years into accountancy in my mother's mind. Anyone who knows me (and especially my accountant!) would know that I would have made a very poor accountant indeed.

Anyway, the point is that projecting your wishes onto the lives of your children can cause a great deal of family friction. Children can feel under pressure to please their parents and comply with their wishes, only to resent it later; or they rebel against their parents' wishes earlier and the parents feel disappointment. Either way, wanting something for someone else is not useful and rarely works out.

> wanting something for someone else is not useful and rarely works out

As parents, of course we are going to have hopes and dreams for our children. What we can do is help them to find out *who they are and what they want* and support and guide them, so that we play a positive part in helping them to create the life they want to lead. They will need encouraging and prodding in certain directions, but we must always ask ourselves who we are encouraging them for, them or us. Is this my dream or theirs? Am I encouraging them to do this because they could be really good at this and they just don't know it yet, or am I encouraging them because I want them to be good at it, for me?

Ask yourself who you want this for – for your child or for you?

It's a fine line to tread.

I remember seeing a well-known actor being interviewed by Michael Parkinson on his television chat show. The actor's mother had recently died and he and his three equally talented and successful siblings had clearly been very close to her. Unprompted, he said that what had made his mother such a wonderful parent was that she always allowed, supported and encouraged them to be themselves and pursue their dreams. It made a huge impact on me; I felt that if my children said that about me, then I would have done a good job.

So what's a good way to think about what we want? The easiest way to think about what we want is to pretend that we are in the future and we already have it or are doing it. In this next exercise, assume that you are your version of a Brilliant Parent, whatever that means to you.

brilliant exercise

You tomorrow

If possible, find a quiet place where you can really concentrate and allow yourself to daydream. Allow about 20 minutes for this if you can.

Now imagine that you are already being the parent you want to be. You are already interacting with your children in the way that you want. You are already behaving in line with your values; you are already managing your emotions in just the way you want to. You are already the role model that you want to be.

Make a list of the positive emotional states, qualities and skills that you want to have as a parent. Use your answers to the questions on page 19 to guide you. Don't hold back – make a good long list.

Spend a few moments thinking about each point on your list, and what it's like for you when you are demonstrating that quality, behaving in that way and feeling that emotion. If 'patience' is on your list, for example, spend a few moments thinking about what it is like when you are being patient, imagine yourself behaving patiently in a situation and so on. Do this with each point until you have thought through each quality.

Make your images vivid – see yourself being the way you want to be, hear yourself and others around you, and feel what it is like.

When you think of your future self, what emotions are attached to that? Positive ones, I would guess. And the more time you spend in that positive emotional state, the more likely you are to do and say the things you want to, to your children.

Now let's step further into the future with the next exercise:

brilliant exercise

The consequences of 'you tomorrow'

Imagine that it is 10, 15 or even 20 years from now and your children have left home. Perhaps they have children of their own. One day you overhear a conversation taking place between one of your grown-up children and a friend of theirs. They are talking about you. Specifically, they are discussing what you were like as a parent; what your parenting did for them.

So you are now in the future listening to this conversation about you.

Write down what they are saying about you – all the qualities they admired in you as they were growing up, how you treated them, what you believed in, what messages they got from you about themselves that helped make them the person they are today.

Now that you have thought through how you are today, how you want to be and the consequences of you making the changes for you and your children, spend a moment comparing 'you today' with 'you tomorrow'. What are the main differences? There may be small differences or there may be bigger differences.

What are the things you want to change?

Making the changes

So how do we get from where we are now to where we want to be?

You have already made the first step by setting yourself a future 'you' to focus on. As it is now in your conscious awareness, it is more likely to happen. Why? Because in your mind, you have already rehearsed being the best parent you can be.

Try the following exercise to keep you focused on the 'future you'. I have found it to work very well as a general exercise to help me to be the best I can be, and it is a good reminder of the person I am trying to become.

⬈) brilliant exercise

You tomorrow

Find a quiet place for this where you will not be disturbed. It will take about 10 to 15 minutes.

Imagine that you have a huge transparent beach ball in front of you that is big enough for you to step inside.

Now imagine that you are placing all the qualities, skills and emotions that you wrote down in the 'you tomorrow' exercise inside that beach ball. Really project them into the ball and fill it up with them.

Next, step inside your imaginary ball and feel all those qualities wash over you and breathe them in. Walk around in your imaginary beach ball for a few minutes. Notice how you are feeling as you walk round. What is different for you?

You may like to do this exercise every now and then to keep it fresh, adding to it or changing it as you wish.

Not only is this exercise very good for keeping you focused on your goals, it can help you to feel more able to handle difficult situations. Every time you are in a situation that you might find difficult with your children, just imagine stepping into your giant beach ball.

brilliant tips

- Remember that we are all 'work in progress' and always learning.
- Revisit the 'you today' exercise and notice what changes you have made.
- Spend a few seconds each morning reminding yourself of 'you tomorrow'.
- Use the beach ball exercise to keep focused on your future self.

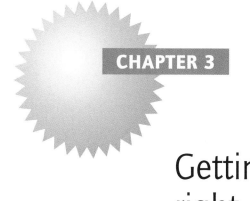

CHAPTER 3

Getting into a right state

B
rilliant parents manage their emotions effectively.

My experience of motherhood so far is that the main thing that stands between how I am now and my version of the mother I want to be, is the ease with which I lose my cool. I'm convinced that my children know exactly what irritates me and do it on purpose!

You probably find that your children are testing you all the time, no matter what their age – and it's tiring. It starts with tantrums when they are tiny and it progresses to different types of behaviour until they leave home (and may well not stop there). They test us because they need to know what they can get away with and what they can't get away with. They need to know the boundaries of behaviour and they test their parents because it's safest for them to test their behaviour on someone who loves them, unconditionally.

As a result of being tested in this way, people who have never got into arguments in their lives and who avoid conflict at all cost find that when they become parents they start shouting like some sergeant major on the recruiting ground. We respond in ways that surprise us sometimes – I never would have imagined getting as angry as I do occasionally, before I became a mother.

One of the reasons we react in this way is the strong emotional attachment that we have to our children. It is much harder to stand back and think rationally when we are embroiled in an altercation with someone we care so much about.

> reacting in negative and uncontrolled ways to our children isn't useful

Losing our cool or reacting in other negative and uncontrolled ways to our children isn't useful. If you can learn to manage your emotional state more effectively when your children or situations press the red button, you'll find it enormously useful.

There are all sorts of things that children do that trigger unwanted emotional reactions in parents: tantrums, ignoring you, not doing what you ask, fighting with siblings, generally behaving badly, not doing homework, refusing to get up for school, leaving their clothes all over the floor and so on. These emotional responses lead us to do or say something that, in more rational moments, we absolutely know is not going to resolve the problem in the long term. We are reacting in the moment, and that doesn't allow for rational thought.

Then, of course, this will start to create more problems. For example, if you shout at your children because they don't listen to you, they get used to it and begin to react *only* when you shout; they don't hear you when you speak at a normal volume. This will probably make you even more frustrated. Of course, children aren't just reacting to you, they are learning from you in every moment, so they'll start to shout at each other at the slightest provocation.

How do we get into a state?

Just as you took some time to think about how you currently behave with your children, let's look in more detail at the states that you get into that you know aren't useful (and how you get into them in the first place).

In order to do that, first take a look at your answers to the 'You today' questions on page 19. What did you write down about what you do that you want to stop doing or do less often?

It might be shouting, as in the above example, or saying things that you later regret, or becoming tearful, or something else.

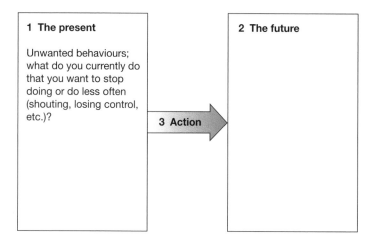

1 The present

Unwanted behaviours; what do you currently do that you want to stop doing or do less often (shouting, losing control, etc.)?

3 Action

2 The future

Now think about what happens *before* you do those things – the more aware you are, the more control you have.

Emotional state affects behaviour

In fact it would be more accurate to say that our behaviour is entirely dependent on, and the result of, our emotional state. I will show you how you can change your emotional state by thinking differently and how you can teach your child to do the same. Imagine how useful it would be if you could help them to feel confident instead of anxious before an exam, for example.

But first let's look at how we get into a negative state in the first place.

Something sets us off: a trigger.

A trigger can be a situation, something we see, something someone else says or does, or even just a sound. Sometimes the trigger sets off a state so quickly that it seems to bypass any thought process at all and the emotion feels out of our control. At other times, the trigger makes us think about certain things, which in turn make us feel a certain way.

So the order of events is: **trigger–(thoughts)–emotional state–behaviour**.

We are going to pay attention to the trigger and the state for now.

In the example of shouting at the children, the trigger could be the children ignoring several requests for them to do something, or it could be a certain look they give you.

The emotional state that is triggered is anger, which then in turn sets off the unwanted behaviour – in this case, shouting.

On the other hand, we can all think of times when we were in such a good mood that even a tantrum didn't shake it and we probably reacted to the situation in a totally different way. As all behaviour leads to consequences of some sort, we get different consequences, too.

brilliant question

Think of a time when you were in a really good mood and reacted differently to a negative situation. What were the consequences?

So how do you break the cycle and maintain an emotional state that is useful to you and your relationship with the children? If you feel angry, how do you snap out of it?

The first step is to work out what it is that is actually triggering your anger (or whatever emotional state we're thinking of). The triggers can be very personal and the answer won't be the same for all people – the same emotion can be triggered by very different things. Let me give you an example.

Speaking in public is a very common fear. What actually triggers the fear may be very different. For some it might be the invitation to speak in public, for others it might be actually walking into the room on the day, and for others it might be even getting out the clothes they intend to wear.

Here's something that happened to a friend and her daughter recently:

---

brilliant example

Jemma's story

Jemma, aged eight, and her mother, Susan, came home from school on their own one afternoon – Jemma's sisters were out for tea. Her mother was looking forward to spending the short time left at the end of the afternoon with Jemma on her own – it was rare that they got to be on their own together and they usually had a lovely time. Jemma was very high spirited that afternoon, in a very positive state, because she had spent the day on a school trip to a museum and had learned about Florence Nightingale, who she thought was amazing.

Susan seized the opportunity to suggest Jemma should do her homework. Oh how quickly things can change! That was the end of the good mood!

First, Jemma suddenly decided that she was fed up that she wasn't out at a friend's for tea. Then she decided that she was not going to do her homework. Susan made gentle attempts to persuade her. She tried to be patient and kept trying to coax her, but the longer Jemma ignored her, the more Susan could feel the tension building up inside her.

Susan started to get cross and reacted, perhaps unreasonably, by angrily packing away Jemma's homework for the night.

So far, the *trigger* was Jemma ignoring her, the *state* was frustration and the *behaviour* was packing away Jemma's homework. Of course, straight away Susan knew how ridiculous it was of her to pack away Jemma's homework, as it needed to be done!

Here's how the afternoon continued. Jemma reacted against Susan by immediately getting out her homework and starting it. But, as she was so cross by now, she didn't read the instructions and so spent the first five minutes answering questions incorrectly. This was followed by equally cross rubbing out.

Jemma also completely ignored all offers of help. As her first round of being angry was triggered by Jemma ignoring her, Susan's anger was ignited all over again except that now it was anger mixed with frustration and then more anger directed at herself for losing her temper so easily. What a catalogue of events over something so small!

What was particularly frustrating for Susan was that she knew that if she had kept patient and light-hearted in the face of Jemma's mood, the afternoon would have been very different.

In this example, there are several rounds of trigger–state–behaviour. The triggers are obvious. Sometimes we just don't know what makes us feel a certain way. There is always *something* that sets it off; it's just that we don't always realise what it is.

So the first step in changing your behaviour is to become aware of the things that trigger your negative states.

> the first step in changing your behaviour is to become aware of the things that trigger your negative states

Let's go on a hunt for some of your triggers. The easiest way to do it is to start with the situation, then think about the unwanted behaviour and then to work backwards to work out the state and finally the trigger.

How to find the trigger

Situation

Take a moment to think about the situations that you are in with your children where you get into moods that you don't like. These are the moods that then lead to you doing the things you don't want to do any more.

? brilliant questions

Where are you, specifically? Is it in the morning before school; are you helping to do homework; are you trying to leave a friend's house after going for tea; are you in the car on the way home from school; is it a meal time or bedtime?

Make a list of all the situations and then choose *one* of these situations to think about as you answer the next questions.

State and behaviour

? brilliant questions

What happens in that particular situation? What is the state that you get into and the behaviour that you exhibit?

Sometimes it is easier to start with the behaviour and work backwards, as in the following example.

▶ **brilliant** example

Pam's story

Pam has a daughter of nine, Lucy. Every morning Pam finds it a struggle to get her out of the house in time for school. Actually, they are rarely late, but Pam ends up feeling frazzled and has spent 40 minutes shouting at Lucy to hurry up. Pam is really fed up with doing this every morning; she goes to work irritable and she really wants to start the day more positively for all their sakes.

- *Situation*: Each morning getting ready for school.
- *State*:
- *Behaviour*. Shouting at her daughter and as a result feeling frazzled.

In Pam's example, we don't know yet what state she is in just before she starts shouting – or what causes her to get into the state. We know what state she is in *afterwards* – frazzled!

Now we can ask Pam what state she was in *just before* she started shouting. Was she angry, frustrated, tired, or something else?

Here's what she told me about the situation. Her daughter is very easy going and relaxed about life. Pam is very organised and busy. Each morning, Pam asks Lucy to get up at a certain time in order to be ready for school. Each morning, Lucy gets up in her own time and gets dressed very slowly. Pam then thinks they are going to be late, and starts imagining all the consequences of being late. She really doesn't like being late, so her thoughts start to make her feel angry, stressed and agitated. The more agitated she becomes, the more she shouts at Lucy, who still gets dressed at her own pace and manages to be ready just in time for school.

So now we have:

- *Situation*: Each morning getting ready for school.
- *State*: Angry, stressed and agitated.
- *Behaviour*. Shouting at her daughter and as a result feeling frazzled.

But what actually *triggered* Pam's stressed and agitated state?

It was *seeing Lucy getting ready at her own pace* and not Pam's pace, and imagining that they were going to be late (thoughts) that set off Pam's state.

Going on the hunt for the trigger

? brilliant question

A question to help you become aware of how your states are triggered is: what did you see or hear, just before you felt that way?

The trigger will be something that you look at, for example your watch, a certain expression that someone has, or something someone else is doing; or a sound that you hear, like a bell ringing, or a certain tonality in someone's voice. In Pam's example, she saw Lucy getting dressed slowly.

If you can't immediately work out what your trigger is, just keep curious and notice what happens next time you are in that situation.

Here's another example.

▶ brilliant example

Bedtime

It's the children's bedtime. You ask them to go upstairs to get washed and ready for bed. They don't. You ask them again, nicely, and they plead for five more minutes, which you agree to, on the basis that they will definitely go up then. They promise that they will, and carry on playing. Five minutes pass, so you tell them that it is now time they went upstairs as they promised. They start asking for five more minutes again and when you say no, they go on and on giving you reasons why you should let them stay up later. Now your patience just snaps and you feel really angry that they have broken their promise to do what you ask, again. You start shouting at them, and then, as you work yourself up into a frenzy, you start threatening all sorts of sanctions: no television (ever again!) and so on. You hurriedly get them into bed, and they are now becoming upset because you are still angry and you leave them to go to sleep without saying goodnight to them properly.

Of course, they don't go to sleep easily, and you end up wondering how you could have handled the situation differently.

Let's break this example down.

● *Situation*: Bedtime.

● *State*: Angry.

● *Behaviour*: Shouting, which leads to all the other behaviour.

What was the trigger here?

It was the children breaking the promise and trying to get more time. That had become a trigger, because in this case it happened frequently.

 **exercise**

Negative situations

Work through the difficult situations that you identified, separating out the trigger, the state and the following behaviour. You may also like to identify the consequences of your behaviour, as in the examples above.

Here are some questions to guide your thinking:

● What is the situation that you find difficult?

● What happens?

● What do you do that you don't like (behaviour)?

● How are you feeling just before you show the above behaviour (state)?

● What do you see or hear that causes you to feel that way (trigger)?

What do you notice about your own examples? Is there a theme to them? What are the differences? Do you have many unwanted states or just one or two that keep recurring?

What have you learned about yourself from thinking about things in this way?

Another reason why it is useful to know what specifically triggers unwanted states is that it is much easier to change the response to the trigger at that stage, in the next moment, than when you are feeling out of control. Our emotional states are like being at the top of a mountain with a toboggan. When you get into the toboggan, you can still change your mind and get out. However, once the toboggan is in motion, it takes over and you can only compose yourself later.

Imagine someone who has a panic attack when the person they are meeting doesn't turn up on time. The trigger turns out to be looking at their watch. It will be much more effective to change the person's thinking when they look at the watch than to give them breathing exercises to do when they are in the middle of a full-blown panic attack.

? brilliant question

Take another look at your examples and ask yourself this question: what is your role in creating the scenarios that cause you problems?

Let's go back to Pam. Remember that she got very agitated about Lucy getting dressed at her own pace. Pam freely admits that she is frustrated by Lucy doing things her own way and not Pam's way. She is creating her own agitation by imagining that they are going to be late if she doesn't shout at Lucy all morning. Does Pam know for sure that if she left Lucy to her own devices, they would be late? The answer is no, she does not know *for sure*.

How about the bedtime example? To what extent is that mother causing her own anger by thinking that her children (under seven) are going to keep their promise tonight in the face of overwhelming evidence that they will try for another few minutes' playing time? Of course they will. Not only are they young, they sometimes get away with it.

Just as there are situations that we find difficult, let's put some balance into this by thinking about the times when you have a lovely time with your children, when you all have a great time together and there are no cross words. It is useful to know what is going on when things are working just the way you want them to, so that you can do them more often.

⚡ brilliant exercise

Positive situations

Think about positive times and situations and work them through in just the same way as you did with the difficult situations. Where are you? What's happening? How are you feeling? How are you communicating with the children? What is the response you are getting from them? And, most importantly, what is it about the situation that causes you to be in a good and resourceful state? What happens in those situations when one of your children does something that would usually trigger a negative state in you?

For example, sometimes you may pick up the children from school or child minder and, since you have had such a good day, their bickering just passes you by, and you deal with it in a totally different way. What label would you give to a state like that?

What states do you experience in your life now, which enable you to behave in just the way you want to with your children?

Make a list of the situations, states and behaviours that you currently enjoy and like in yourself. Use your original answers to guide you. Don't confine your answers to times with the children – use other examples, too. For example:

● *Situation*: Taking them on a picnic.

● *Trigger*: Watching them having fun.

● *State*: Relaxed, peaceful and happy.

● *Behaviour*: Responding to them in a calm tone, saying yes to their requests and having simple fun with them.

Again, what do you notice about these answers? Are there any patterns? What is similar or different about the triggers?

Now you have a list of situations, triggers, states and behaviours that are positive and negative for you. If we were to put it into the Brilliant Framework and summarise it under headings it would look like this:

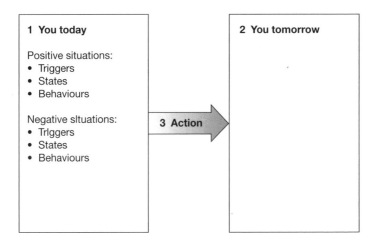

And here's a simple but incomplete example of what might be written in it:

► brilliant example

Positive and negative situations

Positive situations:

- *Triggers*: Watching them play nicely, planning a day out, hearing about something they've learned at school and are excited about, listening to certain music, running.

- *States*: Calm, playful, relaxed, proud, energised.

- *Behaviours*: Smiling and helpful, listening and making time, focused.

Negative situations:

- *Triggers*: Being ignored, children not keeping promises, a certain look.

- *States*: Angry, resentful, frustrated.

- *Behaviours*: Shouting, getting upset, being unsupportive with homework.

You are probably already thinking about how to create more of the positive states and fewer of the negative ones, using this information.

Brilliant strategies for making changes

You will, by now, be more aware of what you do – which in itself will mean that you focus more on what you want and less on what you don't want. Here are some other ideas:

brilliant tips

- If possible, avoid the triggers that trigger negative states.
- If not, notice your part in bringing on your negative state and do something different in the moment, however small.
- Think of ways to recreate the situations that trigger the positive states; for example, ask your children more questions about what they learned at school if that triggers a positive state in you.
- Practise getting into positive states *before* a situation or time you find difficult. Listen to upbeat music before the children's bedtime; or think of your favourite place in the world and imagine being there, before you do the school run.
- Do the beach ball exercise (page 26).

It is *much* more effective to change your state than try to *do* something differently. Remember, state affects behaviour, so if you change your state, you change your behaviour. There are other ideas on how to change state for you and your children in Chapter 7.

Finally, in this chapter, before we move on to your children, let's revisit the 'you tomorrow' – what you want. Being very specific about what you want, particularly in relation to you and your states and subsequent behaviours, is a very effective way to create change.

brilliant exercise

You tomorrow

Remember your beach ball? Have another look at the list of qualities, skills and states that you have and want to have to be the parent you want to be. Add any more that you missed previously.

Your beach ball list might include:

- happy
- relaxed
- calm
- playful
- kind
- understanding
- generous of spirit
- patient
- loving
- sense of humour
- curiosity
- fair
- consistent.

Now imagine your beach ball with the 'future you' inside it. Get a really good sense of watching yourself having all those qualities. Make it sparkly if you like, just for fun; use your imagination and pile on the qualities.

What happens if I do respond emotionally?

brilliant example

Isabella's story

Isabella is six and has a habit of losing control of her temper when she can't make a decision. On this particular day, it was about what to wear. Her family were going out for the day and her mother had given her three choices of clothes. Her mother had previously found that that could be successful, and she believed that it was important to give her children choices over small things so that they learned how to make decisions. Isabella started to lose her temper about the clothes; she didn't know which ones to choose and she got herself into such a state about it that everyone else in the family lost their patience pretty quickly. When Isabella gets into that state, it is difficult for her to get herself out of it, and she gets worse and worse, shutting herself into her room, shouting at her parents if they try to help and refusing to cooperate.

Given that this behaviour is unacceptable to her mother, her mother gets very cross, very quickly. Isabella usually behaves well but has a very wilful streak. Her parents have had some success in reducing the frequency of these tantrums with star charts and other behavioural techniques, but her mother is absolutely sick of dealing with it and thinks that Isabella is too old for tantrums. She was so angry that Isabella was making them late, that she threatened to put her into the car in her underwear, and then told her to get out of her sight until she calmed down.

All this escalated Isabella's tantrum and her mother's anger.

It is at this place in the story that Isabella's mother lost control of her responses; she started to say things that she would later regret. She told Isabella that she was glad to be going away on business so that she wouldn't have to see her, that she would speak to someone to see if they could have Isabella for the summer so that she couldn't go on holiday with the family, and that she had had enough of her.

She told me that she knew in the moment that she shouldn't be saying those things, but she was just so angry that she felt she almost couldn't help herself. Her anger was a mixture of exasperation, embarrassment that her child was behaving in such a spoilt way, and anger at herself for handling the situation so badly. She said that her reaction was as if she was also a child reacting to her daughter.

Finally, they got out of the house, dressed and ready.

The fact is, however hard we try, there will still be times when we react emotionally rather than respond rationally. It may be because we are tired, worried or have just been pushed once too often that day.

Experiences that are charged with emotion are filed as memories in their raw emotional state unless we are able to rationalise them and code them in a more conscious way. It is fine to file away the memories if the emotion is a positive one, and not fine if it is a negative one. It is the reason that talking things through helps us to feel less emotional because we start to make sense of the experience. It is not necessarily the experience that leaves emotional scars, but how the experience is dealt with or not dealt with afterwards.

Only 50 years ago it was thought that the best course of action for a child who lost a parent was to not include them in any grieving. I know people in their fifties who were not even given an explanation, and left to play on their own while all the adults gathered round to discuss the funeral in hushed tones. It was genuinely believed by some that children wouldn't understand death and so it was better to say nothing at all. The experience of living through the loss for these children is still extremely raw in later adult life.

> the process of understanding enables children to move through an experience

That approach is considered unthinkable now, as it is precisely the process of understanding – making sense of an event – that enables children to move through an experience and carry on with their lives. Now, it is more likely that children who suffer loss get support and counselling to help them make sense of the experience and move forward.

We probably all had experiences as a child, big or small, that are still raw memories. It may be something that now seems ridiculous or insignificant but it still remains as a difficult memory. Perhaps a friend's parent got angry with you for something that wasn't your fault, or a teacher showed you up in front of the class in a way that you didn't understand, or you were picked on by someone and no-one dealt with it. The point is, the memory is more likely to stay as a memory with emotions attached to it if you don't or can't make sense of the experience. Human beings are constantly trying to make meaning of situations, so not understanding something causes us stress.

When children can't make sense of a situation, they make up the meaning. They interpret a situation for themselves to make it make sense. Sometimes their interpretations are the cause of distress for them. For example, it is very common for children to blame themselves when their parents' marriage breaks down.

It is very important therefore to help your child to understand and make meaningful interpretations of interactions with you and others, in a way that is useful for them.

brilliant tip

Listen out for things that your children have misinterpreted and spend some time making sure that they understand what is really happening.

brilliant example

Isabella's story (continued)

Luckily, Isabella's mother realised that she needed to talk through what had happened that morning so that she could minimise the negative effect of her words. Here's what she did:

When she had calmed down, she sat down with Isabella. She used the Brilliant Parent thinking model to guide her thinking. She told Isabella that they needed to make sure that they didn't do that again to each other.

▶

The present

Isabella's mother took responsibility for her emotions and apologised for saying things that she did not mean. She explained that she was so angry that she felt like saying those things at the time. She explained what Isabella had done that had made her so angry. She also explained that it was Isabella's *behaviour* that she didn't like, *not* her as a person, so that Isabella would not get a negative message about her personality.

She helped Isabella understand and take responsibility for her bad behaviour. She told her that she would not be able to have friends round for two weeks and she would get the same punishment if she did it again.

Isabella apologised to her mother for behaving so badly and they both agreed that it must not happen again.

The future

They started to think about what they *wanted* to happen in relation to getting dressed and going out.

Summary

In this chapter you've thought about the situations that you enjoy and the ones you like less; the states you get into, positive and negative, and what triggers those states; and you have considered ideas for making changes.

You have hopefully gained a better awareness of yourself. Now it's time to turn your attention to your children.

brilliant tips

- Notice what things trigger your negative states and try to avoid them if possible.

- If you can't avoid them, do something different in the moment.

- Notice what things trigger positive states for you and remind yourself of what that feels like.

- Practise getting into a good state *before* you have to do things you don't like.

- Spend a few moments imagining everything going really well.

- Do the beach ball exercise.

- If you do respond in an emotional way, spend time afterwards talking it through to make the situation make sense.

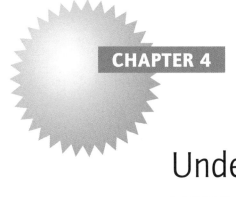

CHAPTER 4

Understanding your child

B rilliant parents take the time and trouble to understand their children as much as they can.

I'm sure that you already know what your children are good at and less good at, what they like and dislike, what they enjoy at school and what they don't enjoy.

This chapter is concerned not with these, but with understanding how your child thinks.

When we understand our children's thinking processes, we can:

- help them become aware of how they create their problems;
- help them become aware of how they succeed at some things;
- help them to learn easily;

- help them to think positively and get what they want;
- use language that gets results.

There are three parts to understanding our children's thinking processes:

- understanding *what* they are thinking;
- understanding *how* they are thinking;
- understanding how the 'what' and 'how' work together to form a strategy.

In order to be able to do this we need to watch, listen and ask questions. A prerequisite for watching and listening effectively is the ability to put aside your judgements.

In the words of one of the most inspirational teachers I know: 'You must keep listening and observing all the time. Don't form an opinion and then only listen to yourself.'

1 Understanding *what* they are thinking

As human beings, the only way we can make sense of other people's experience is through our own experience. 'I know what you mean' is a common and accepted expression. Except that more often than not we don't know what they mean. We can only guess. We all have our own unique internal dictionary, which allows us to make sense of what someone is saying to us, according to our own experiences.

How often have you misunderstood someone because you simply haven't asked them what they mean? Have you ever shared a flat? Was your definition of 'tidy' the same as your flat-mate's?

brilliant exercise

Same words, different meaning

How do your versions of the following words compare with those of your husband/wife/partner/friend?

Both answer the question, 'What do you mean by [fun, and the other words below]?' or 'How would you know that something was [fun]?', and compare your answers. Go through some or all of the following words (you can add your own words too):

- well-behaved
- tidy
- naughty
- discipline
- fun
- adventure
- sharing.

Try asking the questions again when they answer, until you have a really good idea what they mean. For example:

Me: *What do you mean by tidy?*

Friend: *I like things to be put away.*

This is still too vague, so we ask the question again.

Me: *What do you mean you like things put away?*

Friend: *I like totally clear surfaces.*

Now I know. I also know they wouldn't want to live with me, as my version is a bit different to theirs!

Once you have done the exercise, what were the differences in your answers? What were the similarities?

Here's another example.

You might tell me that you like to go to the theatre. In your mind is *what you mean by that statement*: your thoughts of your experiences in your life that add up to 'I like going to the theatre'. On the surface it seems obvious what you mean by that statement.

Because it appears obvious, I will use my version of what I would mean by that statement to book tickets at the theatre.

I present you with some surprise theatre tickets for *Hamlet* in the West End of London. Oh dear. What you meant by 'I like to go to the theatre' was that you like to go to the local theatre to see light-hearted plays or comedies.

So, if you want to know more, the most effective way is to ask '*What* do you like about going to the theatre?'

When we ask the question it is useful to think of it in terms of uncovering the information that the speaker has in their mind at the time – their personal meaning.

Let's consider this example again: 'I like going to the theatre'.

What information is missing? This information, at the very least, is missing from that one small statement: what I like about it, which theatre, when I like to go, how often and what kind of show I like.

So useful questions to ask to avoid assumptions if you were planning some tickets would be any of these:

- What do you like about going to the theatre?
- Which theatre do you like going to?
- When do you like going to the theatre?
- How often do you like to go to the theatre?
- What do you like to see at the theatre?

All these questions are asking for information behind the other person's *actual statement* – this information is their internal dictionary. The questions all use the words of the statement.

Using words from the statement keeps the speaker in their original thought. We make communication much more difficult if we change other people's words into our words when we are trying to understand them.

As an example of what I mean by this, consider this question, which is perfectly relevant to the theatre conversation:

Me: *I like going to the theatre.*

Q: *What did you see when you last went to the theatre?*

In order to answer that question, I will have to access a totally new memory. There is nothing wrong with asking a question like that in conversation, of course. But we need to be aware of how we direct the thinking of the other person with every question we ask.

If your intention is to fully understand the other person's current thoughts, then the quickest and most effective way to do that is to keep the questions phrased around the other person's statement and use their exact words. As a result of using their exact words, your questions may sound a bit clunky to you, and may not be grammatically correct. It doesn't matter in this context.

When we use someone else's exact words they feel heard and respected and they do not notice the grammar.

> when we use someone else's exact words they feel heard and respected

This takes practice. At first, ask yourself, 'What am I asking them to think about with this question?' before you ask it.

So if you want to understand what lies behind your child's words, you need to do these two things:

- use their words;
- ask them what they mean.

For example:

I want to play	What do you want to play?
School's great	What's great about school?
History's rubbish	What do you mean, history's rubbish?
Can we go on an adventure?	What sort of adventure would you like to go on?
That frightens me	What is it about it that frightens you?

Beware of assuming that you know what your child is experiencing. You need to keep asking them questions until you are sure you fully understand. It is always better to assume that you don't know than to assume that you do.

Essentially what your child thinks is the result of their experience of life, and how they have filtered the information they have received. We all filter information differently, according to our beliefs, values, preferences and all our past experiences. This is why different people attach different meanings to events and why two people can see exactly the same event and interpret it differently.

Being able to access someone's thoughts is the key to understanding their experience. This enables us to either reinforce it where it is helping them achieve success, or help them transform it if it is limiting them in some way.

Here's an example of how this works.

brilliant exercise

School trip

Imagine you are going on a school trip with a class of children – it doesn't matter what age. What is the image that comes to mind? What sounds are associated with the image?

First, your thoughts of the impending imaginary school trip will be informed by any previous experiences of school trips you have had, either as a child yourself, or as a parent helping out. These are your experience filters. Your thoughts will also be filtered through your beliefs about school trips – do you think they are fun, or that it is a liability to take 30 children out on a day trip? And they will also be filtered through your beliefs about yourself in relation to the children: do you think that children behave well or badly on school trips, and will they pay attention to you or not?

- *Scenario 1.* I am going on a school trip. I am imagining a group of happy children, smiling and laughing. They are really excited about the trip so they are noisy; I can hear their laughter in my mind. I am imagining myself learning new things with them and start to wonder what those things might be. I see myself with a small group of interested children, discovering something new. As I am having these thoughts, I start to smile and I get a warm feeling in my chest. I begin to feel excited about the trip.

- *Scenario 2.* I am going on a school trip. I am thinking about a group of children who look like they are on the brink of being out of control. I am not sure that they will pay attention to me if I need to discipline them. I have an image of three boys running off and not being able to get them back. I am running all over the place trying to find them.

As I am having these thoughts, my brow furrows and my breathing becomes shallow. I begin to feel worried about the trip.

What sort of experience are you going to have? How are you likely to behave with the children if you are worried about the trip? How might you behave differently if you are excited and looking forward to it? You are more likely to notice good behaviour from the children if you are being positive yourself, because that is what you are paying attention to.

So, your experience largely depends on what you are thinking about before the trip, because those thoughts determine what you will pay attention to during the trip.

In other words, *you get what you focus on*.

 **tip**

You get what you focus on, so make sure it's something you want.

brilliant exercise

Cinema trip

Here's another example of how our thought processes work. Think of the last time you went to the cinema or perhaps watched a film at home. When you were watching the film, all your senses were involved: you were looking at the film, hearing the soundtrack, and experiencing the emotions that the director wanted you feel. You may also have been aware of other sights and sounds in the cinema: somebody blocking your view or shifting in their seat; people talking or eating popcorn. There will have been other feelings too – was the seat comfortable or not? What was the temperature like in there? And you also may have been aware of smells and, if you were eating, tastes.

Now, as you are thinking about it, you are recalling the memory of the experience. The memory probably has lots of information missing in comparison to the original experience. You will have remembered the things you were paying attention to at the time. Remember, that is what forms your thoughts about the original experience.

If you saw the film with someone else, they will have a different memory of the same experience. We have all had the experience of having been with someone at a certain event and having entirely different memories of it.

So, our memory of any experience is formed according to what we pay attention to, and the things we pay attention to depend on our filters. We make meaning of our experiences according to many things, including our beliefs, values, personal preferences and all our previous experiences – the basis of who we are. Therefore, this memory not only has information missing from it, but is also different from reality.

> our memory of any experience is formed according to what we pay attention to

When we talk about the trip to the cinema, our memory gets changed again, through language. We don't tell people *everything* we can remember about the film, we tell them about the bits that we think will interest them, or a potted précis. In other words, we miss out bits and distort the experience still further.

It really is rather miraculous that we can ever understand each other!

Getting what you focus on

You have already spent some time thinking about the kind of brilliant parent that you want to be. You have imagined yourself behaving just the way you want to, heard yourself talking to your children just the way you want to.

You can do the very same exercise with your children. You can easily teach your child to make pictures in their minds of what *they* want to happen. The more vivid their picture, the more likely it is that it will happen. We do this naturally when we know what we want. My daughter recently came home from school and told me about a school trip that she wants to go on in six months' time. She talked about it as if she was already there, painting a picture of what she thinks the B&B will be like, how many children there will be in each room, what activities they will do, how exciting it will be. There is no doubt in her mind that she will be going on that trip.

Maddie's story

Maddie is 13. She plays hockey and decided to enter the county trials for a place in the county squad. There were 90 girls going to the trials that day. Her mother Karen spent some time with her that morning asking Maddie what she wanted to get from the trials.

Maddie: *I want to wear that county shirt, Mum.*

Karen: *Can you see yourself in that shirt?*

Maddie: *Yes, I can.*

Karen: *Great. Now make the picture really colourful and bright and keep thinking about it all day.*

Maddie went off to the trials buzzing with determination. She was the only one to make the squad.

Harry's story

Harry coaches an under-11 football team. The team didn't do very well last season and the boys were feeling a bit demoralised.

It just so happened that Harry got to hear about the technique of visualising what you want and decided to give it a go.

He took each member of the team aside individually. He asked each boy to make a picture of himself playing really well and was very specific about what he wanted them to think about. He made sure that each boy had mentally rehearsed a winning performance, and ended the visualisation with them celebrating.

During the game he just shouted 'You know what to do: remember your pictures!' rather than the numerous instructions that he would normally shout.

The boys played out of their skins that day and came away victorious.

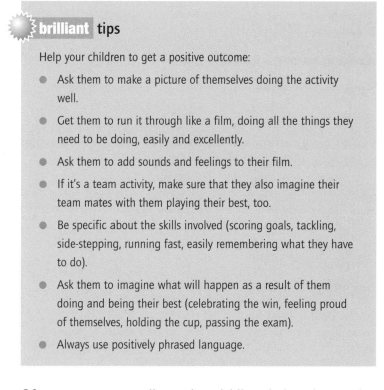

brilliant tips

Help your children to get a positive outcome:

● Ask them to make a picture of themselves doing the activity well.

● Get them to run it through like a film, doing all the things they need to be doing, easily and excellently.

● Ask them to add sounds and feelings to their film.

● If it's a team activity, make sure that they also imagine their team mates with them playing their best, too.

● Be specific about the skills involved (scoring goals, tackling, side-stepping, running fast, easily remembering what they have to do).

● Ask them to imagine what will happen as a result of them doing and being their best (celebrating the win, feeling proud of themselves, holding the cup, passing the exam).

● Always use positively phrased language.

Of course we are equally good at vividly painting pictures that are not helpful to us. We make pictures in our mind that cause us to feel anxious; for example, some of us start 'imagining the worst' if someone we are meeting doesn't turn up on time. We may be making pictures of something going wrong and probably talking to ourselves in a negative way. Often we hear people say, 'But what if I don't pass?' or 'What if they don't turn up to meet me?' In order to say those things they have to have imagined bad things happening. That then triggers a feeling of anxiety. People who spend a lot of time worrying are very good at imagining negative things happening to them and then imagining the next negative event as a result of the first, followed by the consequences of that one. This is not a strategy for a happy life.

brilliant exercise

Worrying about the future

Take a moment to think about something that you were once worried about, or something that you are slightly worried about now. It might be an event that you are organising, something at work or even something small like being concerned that someone will not like the present you have bought them. How are you imagining the future in relation to the issue that is causing you concern? What pictures are you making?

brilliant example

Alice's story

Alice is nearly six and is about to take her first tap dancing exam. She knows all the exercises and routines, has had extra lessons to prepare, has had lots of praise and encouragement from her teacher and even has the music at home to practise in between lessons. Importantly, she has never been under any pressure to take tap lessons because she absolutely loves them and would go to lessons every day if she could.

So imagine her mother's surprise when at bedtime, five days before the exam, Alice started crying and said that she was worried that she might not pass her exam. Her mother's natural response was to comfort her and reassure her that she will pass. That is a response that we all have, but it's not that effective in helping Alice to stop worrying. Telling someone not to worry tends not to work, because the images that are causing them to worry are too powerful.

Alice's mother knew that Alice must be making pictures in her mind, so she asked her, 'What are you thinking about that is making you worry?'

Alice: *I can't tell you.*

Mother: *Can I guess?*

Alice: *Yes, OK.*

Mother: *Are you making pictures of something going wrong?*

Alice: *Yes. I think the examiner will be old and unfriendly.*

Mother: *So what does she look like in your head?*

Alice: *A witch.*

Now that Alice's mother knew *specifically* what was causing Alice's anxiety about the exam, she had lots of choices of how to make Alice feel better. If she had tried to convince Alice that everything was going to be OK because she knew the routines and had been practising, in Alice's mind she would still be performing in front of a witch!

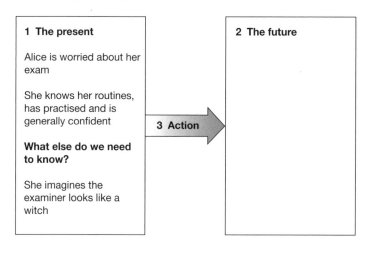

Alice's mother's question 'What are you thinking about that is making you worry?' is an excellent question to find out what is happening now. As with this example, we quite often have to coax the answer from our child in order to move on. Over time, they will get used to the questions and be more aware of their own processes. When they volunteer information like this, you have made significant progress. You have helped them gain personal awareness that will always help them deal with problems in the future.

Getting over anxious moments

Here are some simple ways of getting rid of the anxiety and worry. They are easy to teach to children, too. My children use these strategies on their own now, consciously, if they are worried about something.

All these ideas involve changing, in some way, the thoughts that are creating the negative state that we call anxiety or worry.

Make an image of the event going well

If someone is dreading a presentation, it is common for them to make images of a stoney-faced or heckling audience! Instead they can replace this image with a smiling and applauding audience.

Try it out for yourself. What's the difference in the feelings that are attached to both pictures?

Or, they may have an image of themselves metaphorically going to pieces. They can change that image to one where they look and sound confident and relaxed.

If one of my children is a bit anxious on their way to school or going out somewhere, I ask them to get a picture in their head of them skipping happily into school or enjoying the trip. It has an instant effect.

Make the negative image comical in some way

The solution for Alice and her anxiety about her examiner looking like a witch was to turn the witch into a giant teddy bear! Of course, Alice knew that her examiner wouldn't be a giant teddy, but her new thoughts made her smile and therefore she felt different. End of anxiety.

---

brilliant example

Harry Potter and the Prisoner of Azkaban

J. K. Rowling demonstrates this technique in *Harry Potter and the Prisoner of Azkaban*. In the children's lessons they learn how to deal with their darkest fears. There is a creature called a Boggart whose true form can never be seen because as soon as it comes in front of you it turns into the thing you fear most. So if you fear spiders, it turns into a giant spider. The young witches and wizards are taught to imagine a comical change taking place to the manifestation of their deepest fear while they cast a spell on the creature: 'Riddikulus!' If they imagine hard enough, the creature in front of them will take on the comical changes. So the giant spider suddenly has roller skates. For any Harry Potter fans out there, it is easy for their parents to suggest to them that they make some comical change to the image that is causing them concern.

Push the image away

Sometimes it is the vivid and close-up nature of the image that is frightening for children.

When my son was three years old he started watching Disney videos. I have always been careful about what he watches as he has always been easily frightened by the smallest thing. In one particular week, he watched a bit of *Snow White and the Seven Dwarfs* every night. He absolutely loved it and I was surprised that he wasn't frightened by some of it.

But one night as he was going to bed, he told me that he kept on thinking about the bit where the wicked queen changes into the old woman and that he couldn't get it out of his head.

I asked him to look at the picture of the queen again. This was a mistake because children of that age are so literal – he started to look all around him saying, 'Where?' My second, and much more successful, attempt was to ask him to look at the picture of the wicked queen *in his head*, which he did straight away without question. I asked him if he could make the picture go further away. What he then did surprised both of us for different reasons: he *literally* pushed the picture away from him with his hand and immediately started laughing. When I asked him what had happened, he said that the queen had fallen over and that she wasn't frightening any more.

⁑brilliant tip

It may sound odd to ask 'What happens inside your head?' but I have found that it makes more sense to younger children than 'mind' or 'thoughts'.

Now, whenever my son has frightening or unpleasant thoughts, he knows he can push them away.

Some variations we have used are: crumpling up the picture as if it were paper and throwing it away; changing the qualities of the picture, for example turning the sound down or putting a silly voice in; and occasionally he asks me to push the picture away 'because your arms are longer than mine'!

Act as if they have control of their images

brilliant example

Tom and Theo's story

Theo and his brother Tom were sleeping in the same bedroom when Tom woke up from a nightmare. Theo woke up with the commotion and gave Tom this advice: 'When that happens to me, I just imagine I have a remote control and I change channels.' It worked.

It is so useful to know how we cause ourselves to worry because then we can do something about it. It seems so obvious when you read about it and take a moment to think it through, but most of our thoughts occur below our conscious awareness. Not only this, but people are always surprised to learn how much control they can have over their thoughts.

> people are always surprised to learn how much control they can have over their thoughts

As soon as you hear your child say, 'I'm a bit nervous about . . .', 'I'm a bit worried about . . .', you can be confident that they are making pictures of the future event going wrong in some way.

A lot of our children's day-to-day problems can be overcome just by knowing that this is how we make ourselves anxious. All you need to do is find out what specifically they are thinking about that is causing them to feel anxious and then help them to change the image in some way.

How fantastic to be able to teach your child this skill now.

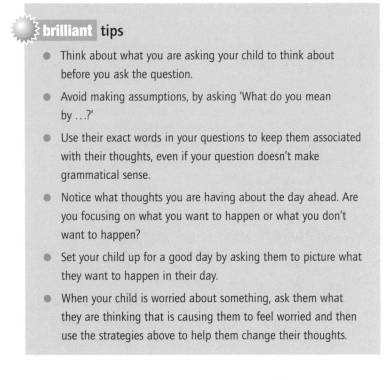

- Think about what you are asking your child to think about before you ask the question.

- Avoid making assumptions, by asking 'What do you mean by …?'

- Use their exact words in your questions to keep them associated with their thoughts, even if your question doesn't make grammatical sense.

- Notice what thoughts you are having about the day ahead. Are you focusing on what you want to happen or what you don't want to happen?

- Set your child up for a good day by asking them to picture what they want to happen in their day.

- When your child is worried about something, ask them what they are thinking that is causing them to feel worried and then use the strategies above to help them change their thoughts.

2 Understanding *how* they are thinking

Your thoughts can be made up of images, sounds, feelings, tastes and smells. Think about your last trip to the cinema. What do you remember most: the images, the soundtrack or the emotions it elicited in you? If people ask me about the soundtrack in a film, I have to confess that I can't remember it – I simply don't notice it as much as the dialogue or the emotions I experienced. So we filter our experiences through our senses too.

It is *how* you are thinking as well as *what* you are thinking that is interesting here. Which senses do you pay most attention to?

We all think in all senses. It is important that we remember this, so that we are not tempted to put our children into pigeon holes that are not useful to them. You may notice that every time they tell you about a new experience, they tell you in a different way, in which case they have a very sensory-rich internal world. Or, you may start to notice that your child demonstrates a particular preference – they always report what they heard, or what they saw for example.

How is this useful? Any insight into how your child thinks is useful for helping them learn, and for simply communicating better with them.

brilliant example

Charlie's story

Vanessa has a five-year-old son, Charlie. She has found it difficult to persuade him to eat certain things, and she has a particularly difficult time persuading him to get into the bath. Charlie seems to be very musical, probably with perfect pitch. When she learned about preferences for certain senses, Vanessa had an insight that helped her speak to Charlie in a way that is very compelling for him.

Vanessa realised that Charlie prefers to use his auditory sense – he likes and is sensitive to sounds, and they are what he pays most attention to. She planned to try some new ways of persuading Charlie to get into the bath and to eat his food. She bought food that made noises and also got some new noisy toys for the bath. When we next met, she was extremely excited about the difference these tactics had made. She found that she only had to say to Charlie, 'Hop into the bath and tell me what the water sounds like when you shake that toy', for him to jump in! The same thing happened with food – Vanessa decided to buy food that was crunchy or made noises. She was amazed by the positive reaction to: 'Charlie, try that new vegetable and tell me what noise it makes when you chew it.' New foods have become irresistible!

▶ brilliant example

Joe's story

Joe is a very active boy, always on the go. He finds it hard to concentrate in class because he doesn't like sitting still. Lots of boys seem to be like this.

His mother was having trouble getting him to sit down to do his homework. I talked to her about these sensory preferences and she realised that he demonstrated a high kinaesthetic preference (to do with your body and movement and touch, as opposed to sounds or visual preferences). They now approach homework in a totally different way.

Joe walks around while reading, he learns his spellings and times tables on the trampoline and his mother does as much as she can to engage him physically in his homework.

As a result, they both have more fun and Joe gets through his homework successfully.

There are three main modes of thinking:

● visual – thinking in pictures
● auditory – thinking in sounds
● kinaesthetic – thinking in feelings or describing actions.

We need to have the open-mindedness that I talked about in Chapter 1: that is, to be non-judgemental and truly interested, if we are going to become more aware of our children's preferences. So how do you determine what sense a child prefers to use, if indeed they have a preference? You need to observe:

● their language
● what they pay attention to.

Listen to their language

How does your child describe their day at school? Do they talk about what things look like or sound like, or do they tell you about the activities?

● *Visual language.* If a child is using visual language, they will use words that visually describe something. For example:

A big tree fell down in Grandma and Grandpa's garden. It had lots of branches poking out and had a greenish trunk. It squashed the pink flowers in the flower bed. We made a bonfire that was really tall with all the thin sticks and branches. The flames were bright orange and the smoke billowed out of the top.

● *Auditory language.* When a child is describing something with auditory language, they will describe sounds and report speech. For example:

Grandpa cut the tree up with a chain saw. It was so noisy. It sounded like a motorbike. Grandma told us to stand a long way back to keep safe. When Grandpa lit the bonfire it really crackled.

● *Kinaesthetic language.* When a child is describing something kinaesthetically, they will talk about what things they did and how they were feeling. For example:

I was helping Grandpa to pick up the sticks and logs. And then I helped Grandma rake the leaves. And I went to the menders to fix Grandpa's electric saw. And I went in the wheelbarrow to the bonfire to put the logs on the bonfire. It was really fun and hard work.

What do they pay attention to?

Here are some other clues to help you work out your children's preferences.

● *Children who have a visual preference*:
  – Do they notice immediately if you are wearing something new or if you've moved the furniture around?

- They can probably tell you where your keys are when you've misplaced them.
- They like things explained in pictures.

● *Children who have an auditory preference*:
- They probably love music and notice noises that other people don't.
- They may need quiet surroundings to concentrate or they may find some places too noisy.
- They tell you about what people have told them.

● *Children who have a kinaesthetic preference*:
- They may be very physical, enjoy sport and are fidgety if they have to sit still for long.
- They possibly have difficulty learning certain things at school if they don't have an opportunity to *do* something during the learning.

brilliant questions

What preferences do your children demonstrate? Do they *predominantly* think in pictures or sounds or do they prefer to act something out? Do they perhaps talk to themselves a lot?

Remember not to pigeon-hole your children. We all use all of these systems. Labelling your child as 'visual', 'auditory' or 'kinaesthetic' is not necessarily helpful. I worked with a teenager who was told that she doesn't visualise. She accepted this statement because it was made by a professional and it has caused her all sorts of problems. As a result of believing that she doesn't visualise, her ability to write creatively has suffered because, for her, she needed to use her imagination (visual) in order to generate ideas for writing.

Everybody visualises to some degree, even if they think they don't. In fact, strangely, it seems to be the very people who think they don't visualise who have a strong visual preference. It's just that they make pictures really fast and they are below conscious awareness. So if your child is really unaware of

everybody visualises to some degree, even if they think they don't

their imagination, you'll need to try asking for the information in creative ways that your child will understand.

Asking questions

Another very effective way of finding out how your child processes information is to ask them questions.

▶ brilliant example

Dylan's story

Dylan is seven. His mother, Louise, always asks him, 'How was school today?' His answer is usually 'Fine'. Imagine her surprise when she challenged him one day: 'Dylan, you never tell me what you've done at school', and got this answer: 'Well, you don't ask the right questions!'

Louise was totally stumped by Dylan's reply and decided to put more thought into her questions.

The key thing with asking questions is to really consider what we are asking the child to think about. Let's take the example of trying to get information out of our school children.

'How was school?' is much too vague for some children. To answer that question they have to run through the whole day very quickly in their mind. They do not have the capacity to choose one thing to evaluate. It is much more effective for you to choose one piece of the day to ask them about. If you know their preference in sensory-based thinking, start the questions in that sense.

For example, Louise knows that her daughter Morgana has a visual preference and so she starts the questions with, 'Who was sitting next to you at story time?' Morgana gets a picture of the person next to her in order to answer the question. Louise has reconnected her with a specific experience and can now ask for other details that she is interested in hearing about. The first time Louise asked what story the teacher was telling, Morgana repeated the entire thing, reliving the experience.

If you specifically want to guide the answer to a particular sense, try some of the following questions.

- Questions requiring a visual answer:
    - Who did you see at school today?
    - What was your teacher wearing today?
    - What work is displayed in your classroom at the moment?
- Questions requiring an auditory answer:
    - What did you hear about today?
    - What did the teacher tell you about/talk about?
    - What songs did you sing in the music lesson?
- Questions requiring a kinaesthetic answer:
    - What did you do today?
    - What games did you play at break time?

At any time we can also ask questions directly:

- What pictures are you making in your head [*visual*]?
- What are you listening to [*auditory*]?
- What are you feeling [*kinaesthetic*]?

Here's an example of how these questions worked with Dylan.

brilliant example

Dylan's story (continued)

Dylan had come home from school saying that he had had a really good game of football. Normally, the conversation would have ended there. Louise, having thought about what questions would be effective, found herself taking him back to that experience. The result was that Dylan felt fantastic all over again and Louise felt like she had been at the match herself. This is how she did it:

Louise: *Dylan, can you get a picture in your mind of a really good bit of the football match, when you were playing really well?*

Dylan: *Yes.*

Louise: *Can you tell me what's happening?*

Dylan: *Well, I can see myself on the pitch with some of my friends in the team.*

Louise: *So tell me what's happening.*

Dylan then went into great detail about what was happening in that moment as if he were commentating on the match. As he did that, Louise started to ask about the other senses:

Louise: *As you look at those pictures, can you hear anything?*

Dylan: *Oh yes! I can; I can hear all the cheering and the shouting!*

Louise: *And how are you feeling now?*

Dylan: *I feel like I did when it happened – fantastic!*

If we get this quality of information from our children, we can put it to good use.

Louise suggested to Dylan that any time he wanted to feel fantastic like that, he simply had to think of that piece of the football match. That memory will become a trigger for feeling fantastic, which Dylan can access any time he likes. State affects behaviour!

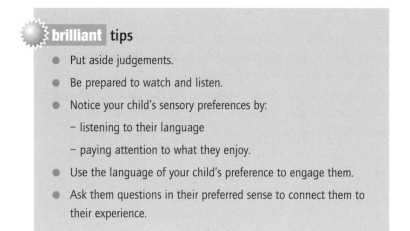

brilliant tips

● Put aside judgements.

● Be prepared to watch and listen.

● Notice your child's sensory preferences by:

– listening to their language

– paying attention to what they enjoy.

● Use the language of your child's preference to engage them.

● Ask them questions in their preferred sense to connect them to their experience.

3 Understanding how they put it all together to form a strategy

We have a strategy for everything we do, whether we know it or not. We have a strategy for brushing our teeth, for getting dressed, for remembering where our car keys are and for more complex tasks. Some of our strategies are very effective and some are less effective.

A strategy really just means *how we do what we do*. It is a combination of the things that we physically do that can be observed by others and what and how we think. All this leads to a result of one sort or another, whether it be successful or less than successful.

we aren't consciously aware of most of our strategies

We aren't consciously aware of most of our strategies, certainly not the thinking part anyway. The strategy is operated at an unconscious level. As a result, if we are really good at something and someone asks us how we do it, the chances are we won't be able to tell them – not easily anyway.

My father was very good at maths. I remember him trying to help me with my maths homework as a teenager. The experience was deeply frustrating for both of us. I simply could not make sense of the way he approached the problems. What I realise now is that his way of thinking through the problems was completely different to my way of thinking. Neither of us was consciously aware of *what* was different in our thinking, and we certainly didn't have the ability to find out. In fact, we weren't even remotely aware of the possibility of understanding each other; we just knew that we did things differently and got frustrated. If only I had known then what I know now.

I would also love to know how some people can look in the fridge and construct a fabulous meal out of whatever is there. I have a friend who can do this. How does she know that it will taste good? How does she know how much of each ingredient to add? How does she know how long to cook it for? . . . All the answers to those questions are in her mind, and very possibly out of her conscious awareness.

When I asked her how she did it, her first reaction was 'Well, everyone can do it', followed by, 'I don't know, I just can', followed by disbelief that everyone can't automatically do it. You see, when someone is very good at something, it is easy for them and so they assume that it must be easy for everyone else.

In sport, psychologists are employed as a matter of course to help players with their 'inner game' – their mental strategy. At the top level, it is, more often than not, the athlete's mental strategy that makes the difference between winning and losing.

The great tennis champion Roger Federer reaches shots that astound commentators, who say that it's not humanly possible to reach shots in that way. Roger Federer says that he does it by 'putting the game into slow motion'. How on earth does he do that? I wonder if anyone knows his strategy for slowing down time.

> to be successful children also need to know what they do less well

For children to be successful in life, they need to be aware of what they do well. They need to know specifically how they do something well so that they can keep improving it and do it more often. But to be successful children also need to know what they do less well. They need to know how they do those things less well so that they can stop doing them or change the way they do them and find a way that works better.

So, as parents, we need to learn how to uncover our children's successful strategies and also their strategies for causing themselves problems.

How to discover a strategy

There are three key steps to any strategy:

1   The starting point or the trigger – what is it that sets the strategy off? How do your children know when to start the strategy?

2   The steps – these are the steps of the strategy that take place inside their mind, and their behaviour.

3   The end of the strategy – how do they know when to stop?

We have already looked in detail at our strategies for getting into a particular emotional state (see Chapter 3). Now we can apply the same thing to understanding our children.

brilliant example

Sam's story

Sam was a typically moody teenager, up one minute and down the next. He was able to go from really enthusiastic to sullen and rude in a moment. His family got pretty fed up with not knowing when he was going into one of his bad moods, and, when he was in one, not knowing how to deal with it. They tried ignoring him, getting cross, and everything in between, including asking him why. They didn't get anywhere, until one day his father tried a different tack.

Here's how he found out Sam's strategy.

Dad: *Sam, you are really good at getting yourself into one of those moods. I am interested,* how *do you do it?*

This question threw Sam into some kind of confusion, but his father persisted with an attitude of genuine curiosity. Sam really had to think about the answer and was surprised himself when he eventually came out with the following:

Sam: *Well, I think about someone I don't like and talk to myself about them.*

Dad: *And then what do you do?*

Sam: *Well, then I look at the ground and walk like this . . .*

At this point Sam demonstrated rounded shoulders and dragging feet.

Dad: *So first you think of someone you don't like, talk to yourself about them, then you look at the ground, then you round your shoulders and drag your feet. Is that right?*

Sam: *[surprised] Yes.*

Try it. It's enough to put anyone into a bad mood!

Sam's father now knows Sam's strategy for getting into a bad mood but he doesn't yet have the trigger – what causes Sam to decide to go into the bad mood in the first place.

If asked the right questions, Sam might be able to become aware of what sets him off. And if he becomes aware of what it is that sets him off, he straight away has more choices in the moment.

The question for Sam is: 'What happens just before you start thinking about . . .?' Or, 'How do you know when to start getting into a mood?' This is Sam's answer:

Sam: *When you ask me to do something I don't want to do.*

Finding out how Sam got himself into such bad moods so often was a breakthrough for the family. It had been extremely tiring for them all to try to manage Sam's moods. Sam also gained new awareness, which opened up choices for him. As he was now conscious of how he created the bad moods, he couldn't really do them as effectively any more because he realised what he was doing and found it amusing!

This new awareness also enabled Sam and his father to have a conversation about Sam's response to requests – a conversation that simply was not open to them before.

brilliant tip

Make sure that you are curious and open minded. It's important that you stay interested and non-judgemental.

So, to go back to our three steps to discover a strategy:

1 *First, we need the starting point.* Ask: 'How do you know when to start . . .?' Or 'What happens just before you . . .?'

2 *Then we need to know the strategy.* Keep the questions simple. Keep watching and listening and prompting when they can't answer. Ask: 'What is the first thing you do . . .?' Or 'What is the first thing that happens?' Or 'What did you do in your head/mind?' Or 'What did you start thinking?'

Keep asking: 'Then what happens . . ?' until you think you have the whole strategy. Repeat their strategy back to them. It should be logical – imagine doing the strategy yourself to see if it makes sense.

3   *Finally, we need to know how they know when to stop.* Most of the time this is obvious and you don't need to ask. Just be aware that there is an end to every strategy. In Sam's case, the end of the strategy is when he is in a very bad mood.

---

brilliant example

Helen's story

Helen (14) was having extra lessons for maths. When the maths teacher asked her what had brought her to these lessons, Helen said, 'I can do the easy sums but not the difficult ones.' There is a great deal of information about Helen's strategy in that one sentence! For example, how does she decide that something is easy or not? How does she decide it's difficult?

Instead of just teaching Helen how to do the difficult sums, the maths teacher did something much more effective. She decided to find out Helen's strategy for doing easy sums.

She asked Helen to do an easy sum on the list. Helen did it immediately and the teacher then asked, 'How did you do that?' Like most of us, Helen had no conscious awareness of her mental strategy, so she replied, 'Well, I just knew it.' Not to be beaten, the teacher explained that we have a strategy for everything, even getting out of bed and cleaning our teeth, and that some of the steps in the strategy are things that we do and some of the steps happen in our mind. She explained that even if you think you just know something, you have been through some very quick mental processes to get there.

So the teacher tried again:

Teacher: *When you look at that sum, what's the very first thing that you do in your head?*

Helen: *Oh yes, I have a picture of the two numbers in my head so that I can decide which one is bigger.*

The teacher carried on with this line of questioning, asking 'And what's the next thing that happens?' and so on until she had Helen's entire strategy written on a piece of paper.

The next step was to try out this strategy on the 'difficult' sums. The teacher asked Helen to choose the most difficult one on the page. Despite protestations from Helen, they methodically applied her strategy to the difficult sum and managed to get to the right answer quickly and easily.

Helen now knew how to do all the difficult sums and had learned how to do it by becoming aware of her own mental processes. How much more motivating and inspiring that is for the child than trying to teach them how to do a 'difficult' sum. Brilliant.

---

brilliant example

Jack's story

Jack, 10, came home from school upset because his teacher told him that he 'Never listens.'

His mother agrees that it is very difficult to get his attention sometimes. And when you do have his attention, it seems to wander while you are speaking to him.

Jack does have a good ear for sound, so I wondered what was going on with his 'selective' hearing.

I spent some time with him asking him about what prompted his teacher to say what she had to him. Evidently, she had sent him down to the school office to get the school stamp and he had returned with a postage stamp!

Jack was also the only one to hand in some homework incorrectly completed because he hadn't listened to the instructions carefully enough.

I have coached an adult before who had the same issue – he had problems listening to people. He had been *taught* how to listen, maintain eye contact, etc., but it hadn't worked for him. Here's why: saying that someone doesn't listen assumes that there is a gap in their skills that just needs filling. This is not the case. If someone is not listening, they are doing *something else*.

My job was to discover these people's strategy for 'not listening'.

In the adult's case, I asked him what he was doing *instead of listening*. He found that question intriguing. He wasn't aware until that moment that he was doing anything at all. When he thought about it he realised that he was thinking about everything else he had to do that day, and rehearsing lists of things to do. When he became aware of that, he had the choice of stopping and engaging with his colleague.

In Jack's case, I asked him: 'When your teacher is giving you instructions, what are you doing when you are not listening?' Well, it turns out that Jack was talking to himself almost constantly. People sometimes call Jack a deep thinker. But what is a deep thinker? It is someone who is asking themselves questions and commentating on their actions. As that is not useful when someone else is talking to you, Jack needed a strategy for turning down this internal dialogue.

I asked Jack to imagine that he had a remote control that he could use to turn down the sound of his own voice in his head. He used it straight away and it really worked well for him.

brilliant example

William's story

William is about to take his Grade 5 cello exam. He loves playing his pieces but will not practise his scales without a fight. He is naturally musical and quickly learns pieces off by heart. His mother has always assumed that he is very auditory in his processing because he can pick out a tune after hearing it. William has always practised his scales without the music, doing it by ear and feel.

One night his mother asked him how he plays the pieces off by heart. He replied: 'I see the music in a cloud and read it from there.'

William's mother had wrongly assumed that he was remembering the sound of the music and the feel of the fingering on the strings. No wonder he couldn't remember the scales.

Now they can use this information to learn and practise the scales from the music until he can 'see the scale in the cloud'.

When you first start to get interested in the inner workings of your child's thoughts, be prepared for some strange answers. When I work with people in my role as their coach, they are often surprised when they realise how they think about certain situations. I wish I had money for every time a client says, 'I never realised I was thinking that – do you think I'm mad?!' ('No' is my answer to them, by the way!)

I once asked a child of about five how he got the very speedy maths answer that he came up with. After a short pause he told me that the little green men in his head run around and bring the right number to the front of his head so he can read it! His little green men are very helpful to him, but I don't think I'll be suggesting sharing that strategy to other people!

Encouraging children to be curious about each other's strategies

Eliciting children's successful strategies is a great way to learn about learning and to get children interested in how we all do things differently.

We were on holiday with some friends and I was with the four children sitting on a wall waiting for someone to join us. To pass the time, one of the children suggested that we did some sums – they were still at the age when adding and subtracting had some novelty! All of them thought it was a great idea, amazingly, so I duly set about firing simple sums at them in turn. Then something happened that surprised and delighted me: one of them asked the others how they did the sum in their head – and they proceeded to elicit each other's adding strategies. And because children are naturally curious, their conversation was peppered with: 'Gosh, I don't do it like that, I do it like this . . .' and 'I'll see if I can do it your way.'

The four children effectively shared their strategies and started to work out which one worked best. Imagine what would happen if that happened in classrooms round the country.

In the next chapter we will focus on problem strategies: examples of how children create problem thinking, and how you can find out about it and help them sort it out.

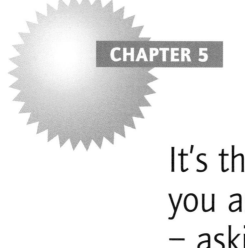

CHAPTER 5

It's the way
you ask them
– asking
brilliant
questions

I f anyone ever wanted proof of the power and value of being able to ask questions, I would remind them of the story of Lindsay and her daughter Corinne. You may remember that Corinne had spent four years suffering acute anxiety, causing her to feel sick and sometimes be sick before school. Corinne finally stopped when she saw the school counsellor, who discovered the cause of the problem through asking simple questions.

Her mother Lindsay said to me, 'It's a shame that nothing I said to her made any difference.' When I pointed out to her that usually it's not what we *say* that makes a difference, it's what we *ask*, she looked at me aghast. 'Oh my God, you're right. I didn't know how to find out.'

One of the key skills of a brilliant parent is being able to ask great questions – and that's what this chapter is about.

> one of the key skills of a brilliant parent is being able to ask great questions

In the last chapter, we touched on the use of simple but effective questions to find out what someone means, so that we can get more information, increase our understanding and avoid making assumptions.

This is just a wild guess, but have you ever had this conversation?

You: *How was school today?*
Child: *Fine.*

Great. The whole day distilled into one non-descript word.

Wouldn't it be lovely if we got an answer like this?

I played football and we won. Charlie got injured during the game and had to go to the nurse. Lunch was horrible; we had soggy vegetables again. Charlotte's invited me to the cinema but I don't really want to go. Our history lesson was good. We did some cool stuff on gladiators and the teacher was really funny.

Sometimes, of course, it is perfectly OK to accept 'Fine' as an answer, but there are other times when it is extremely useful and/or important to find out what lies behind what our children have said. We can use the questions in the last chapter to uncover more information, simply by asking 'What do you mean by fine?'

Here, we will build on those questions to ask the kind of questions that we wouldn't necessarily *ever* think of asking. What follows are the questions that enable you to find out how your child is creating their problem, and how you can help them to think differently.

Questions that unravel problems

It's back to the Brilliant Framework:

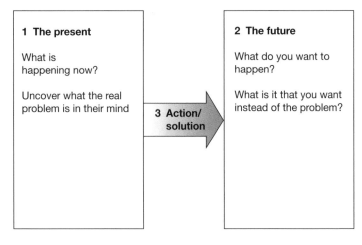

1 The present		**2 The future**
What is happening now?		What do you want to happen?
Uncover what the real problem is in their mind	**3 Action/ solution**	What is it that you want instead of the problem?

Brilliant parents help their children to solve their own problems, rather than offering solutions. They do this through asking them questions that help them unravel the problem, before asking questions to find out what their children want instead. Once your child is clear about what they want, they tend to be able to come up with their own solutions.

Our tendency, particularly with our children, is to offer solutions or comforting words as soon as they mention a problem, because we want to help:

I'm worried about my exam, Mum.	You'll be fine, honestly.
I don't think I have any friends.	Of course you do, that's ridiculous!

We automatically say something to make our children feel better because we care. The thing is, it doesn't work that well because it doesn't change their thinking.

We can't offer really effective help until we know what the problem is.

Sometimes, we are at a complete loss to know what to do to help because what your child says leaves you speechless:

> we can't offer really effective help until we know what the problem is

- Ben comes home and says, 'I don't know what to do because I don't want to let you down.' Do you wonder what you must have said to make your child feel under pressure like that? You know that you have never mentioned that you would feel let down by them and you wonder where it came from.

- Your high achieving but sensitive child comes home and says, 'I don't think anybody notices me.' '*What*?!' you think incredulously. 'How do you think that!?'

- 'I don't think I have any friends.' How do they come to that conclusion when every morning at least three children wait for them at the school gate?

Children make their own sense of the world and sometimes you just won't get it.

Knowing how to ask incisive questions means that we can *always* help in some way. And as we continue to use this strategy, our children begin to learn to question their own problems and think about what they want instead.

Most problems are caused by thinking in a certain way. We hear about them stated in language like the examples above and like this:

- I can't do maths.
- My friends don't want to play with me any more.
- I'm worried about my test.
- I don't want to go to Grandma's this weekend.
- I just don't like school any more.

I ran a workshop once for some sales people where the purpose was for them to come up with some new processes for getting new business. At the end of the day, one of the group said, 'This is all very well, but they won't let us do this.' I immediately wanted to give her the reasons why she would be able to implement the changes, but I realised that asking some questions would be much more effective.

Toni: *They won't let us do this.*

Me: *Who's 'they'?*

Toni: *The Management.*

Me: *Who are 'The Management' who won't let you do this?*

Toni: *[rather sheepishly] Debbie.*

Me: *So Debbie won't let you do this. How do you know that Debbie won't let you do this?*

Toni: *I don't know. I guess I could ask her.*

You will notice that all I was doing was asking her questions that uncovered more and more of her thoughts behind her original statement.

brilliant tip

> To make sure that your questions uncover your child's thoughts, you need to keep being interested in what must be behind the statement in order for it to make sense to the individual and be causing them a problem in some way.

Let's consider some children's examples.

brilliant example

Thomas's story

Thomas came home from school one afternoon when he was about six years old, and told me that the girls in his class play on their own in the playground. He told me more and more details about their games and started to cry. I was rather puzzled as to what the problem was. How did the girls' play affect him exactly? The questions going round in my head were: Did he want to play with them? Was he being left out? Were they being unkind to him in some way? However, these questions would not have been very effective.

Using the Brilliant Framework, I had to focus on the 'the present' first. I needed to find out what he was thinking that was making him upset.

There was obviously a relationship in his mind between the girls playing on their own and him being upset but it was certainly not obvious to me. I wondered whether he had made a connection that the right questions might just unravel. I asked a question that is extremely effective when it is not clear how what a child is saying affects *them*.

Me: *How is 'the girls playing on their own' a problem for you?*

Thomas: *Well, they play their own games.*

I was still none the wiser so I asked the question again!

Me: *And how is their playing their own games a problem for you?*

What happened next surprised me, even though I have witnessed it so many times before in so many contexts.

As Thomas thought about the answer, he realised that it wasn't a problem at all. It just disappeared. He quickly went from upset to puzzled to talking about something else!

 **example**

Laura's story

Laura is seven and is moving up a year at school. She has some good friends in her current class. The school, like many others, shuffles the children up when they move up, so they get to be in a class containing some new faces.

When Laura learns of her new class, she is really upset. Her parents try to find out why and gather that she is particularly concerned about not being with her close friend, Betty. They also guess that she is nervous about sharing a building with the bigger children, some of whom seem huge to her.

Her parents are at a loss as to what to do to help her to feel OK about next term. They tell her that she will make new friends, that her teacher is lovely, that the children aren't really that big, and she really doesn't have anything to worry about.

Laura is still upset.

At this point her parents do not actually know what she is thinking that is causing her to be upset. They are guessing.

What does Laura imagine will happen as a result of her best friend, Betty, not being with her? Without knowing the content of what she is imagining, Laura's parents are having to guess at solutions that they hope will reassure her.

They need to know exactly what she is thinking about that is causing her to be upset before they can really help her.

So how do they find out? They have already asked her *what* is upsetting her, which is a great way to start the questions. (Avoid asking '*Why* are you upset?' because children (and adults) tend to give answers that yield little information.)

Parents: *What is upsetting you about your new class?*

Laura: *Betty won't be with me.*

This is the moment that we usually start unwittingly to read our child's mind and try to help them with 'Never mind, you'll make new friends', etc.

The statement 'Betty won't be with me' is just the surface information, under which lies the reason for Laura's upset – her thoughts in the form of pictures, sounds and feelings.

You will be realising by now that this is an example of anxiety. In other words, Laura will certainly be imagining things happening in the new class that is not what she wants to happen. What is she imagining?

Here are some questions that Laura's parents could have asked her that would give them more information about what she is doing to create her anxiety:

- What do you think will happen if Betty isn't with you?

- When you imagine that Betty isn't with you in the new class, what happens next?

We can carry on asking 'and then what happens?', until we get a really good idea of the problem.

Here's what happened when they asked her more questions:

Parents: *What do you think will happen if Betty isn't there?*

Laura: *Well, I don't really know anyone.*

Parents: *And what happens when you don't really know anyone?*

Laura: *I won't have anyone to talk to when we are doing work.*

So Laura is upset, not because of Betty, specifically, but because she thinks that she won't have anyone to talk to. Now her parents know what she needs.

Laura is making pictures in her mind of doing pieces of work on her own.

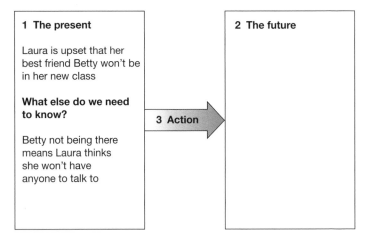

So what does Laura want? She wants to know that there will be someone to talk to when she gets into the new class.

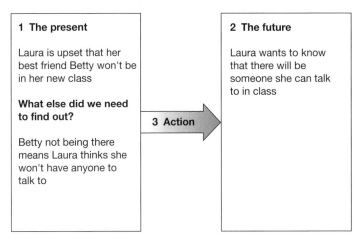

1 The present

Laura is upset that her best friend Betty won't be in her new class

What else did we need to find out?

Betty not being there means Laura thinks she won't have anyone to talk to

3 Action

2 The future

Laura wants to know that there will be someone she can talk to in class

What action can her parents take to make this happen for Laura?

Action

Her mother organised a number of playing visits with the girls in her new class over the summer holidays. Laura got to know three or four of the girls in her new class and started the term feeling confident.

brilliant example

Tom's story

Tom seems to lack confidence sometimes. He is six. He loves football and is desperate to join in with a large group of adults and children. His mum, Pam, is there too, playing in the group, but despite that he will not join in.

Pam can see that Tom really wants to play, and as time goes on he starts to cry and gets into a state on the sidelines. Pam is very encouraging at first, making sure that he really does want to join in, coaxing him onto the pitch with kind words, asking him why he doesn't just run onto the pitch – all to no avail.

As Tom gets more upset, Pam starts to get cross with him, and when that doesn't work either she tells him to either get a grip of himself or go away ▶

because she doesn't want to watch him crying any more. Tom doesn't get to play football, his confidence stays low, and his mother is cross.

Pam tried different approaches, none of which worked, and got cross with Tom because she didn't know what else to do and was so frustrated with the situation. Then she felt bad for ages afterwards.

Pam's frustration was compounded by her lack of personal experience of what it is like to lack confidence. Our children sometimes have such different personalities to us, or behave in ways that we don't understand, that we simply cannot relate to their behaviour. If we can't understand them, we are limited in the help that we can give them. In this case, Tom's mother is very confident and always has been. She simply does not know what it is like to feel the way he does.

So what she needed to find out was *how* Tom was making himself feel unconfident. What was he doing that stopped him from running onto the pitch? No amount of coaxing, cajoling or shouting was going to get him onto that football pitch. Instead, Pam asked more questions:

Pam: *What was it that made you start feeling like this?*

Tom: *I saw a big boy from school get up to play.*

Pam: *What was it about the big boy getting up to play that caused you to feel like this?*

Tom: *I thought he might come up to me and get the ball off me.*

Pam: *What do you think might happen if he got the ball off you?*

Tom: *He would laugh at me.*

Pam: *And what would happen if he laughed at you?*

Tom: *I would cry and more people would laugh at me.*

So now Pam knows how he is making himself so anxious that he can't play football.

At this point it is useful to repeat the whole thing back to the child. Sometimes repeating it back makes the child see things in a different way.

Pam: *So Tom, when you saw the big boy run onto the pitch, you imagined that he might come up to you and get the ball off you. And then you thought that he would laugh at you until you cried and other people would laugh at you, too.*

Now that we know specifically what is causing the anxiety that is preventing Tom from playing football, we have a much better chance of helping him to think differently. We have the piece that makes the difference.

The next step in our questioning is to challenge his internal reality.

Pam: *Tom, how do you know that that big boy will get the ball off you in that way?*

Tom: *Well, he might.*

Pam: *And he might not.*

Tom: *I suppose so.*

Pam: *Tackling people is part of football, so what makes you think that people would laugh at you?*

Tom: *I don't know.*

Pam has created doubt in Tom's mind now about what he thinks will happen.

▶

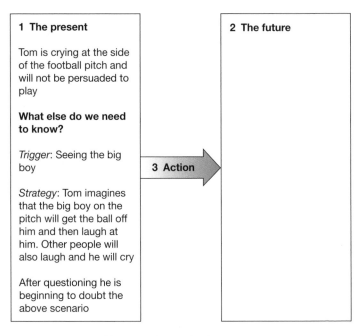

Pam can now start asking Tom about what he wants.

Pam: *What do you want Tom?*

Tom: *I want to play football with everyone.*

Pam: *Are you sure?*

Tom: *Yes.*

Pam was sure that Tom wanted to play football and the thing that was preventing him was his internal representation of the boy and what the boy might do to him.

Action

Tom needed to change the picture. Pam created a new scenario for him to play as a film in his mind.

Pam: *Tom, let's change that picture you have in your head so that you can have some fun. What do you think?*

Tom: *OK.*

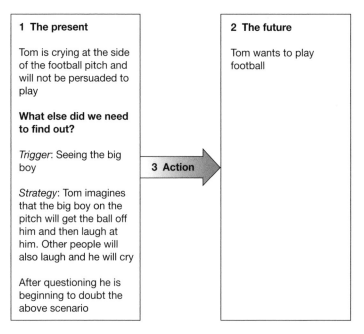

Pam: *Can you make a picture of yourself running onto the pitch and tackling one of the dads and getting the ball off them?*

Tom: *[smiling] Yes.*

Pam: *That would be good, wouldn't it?*

Tom: *Yes!*

Pam: *What else can you imagine happening that would be fun?*

Tom: *I could try to score a goal too!*

Pam: *Very good!*

Pam noticed that Tom's state had changed enough to be in a position to get him onto the pitch. She knew that once he was playing, everything would be fine.

▶ brilliant example

Isabella's story (continued)

You may remember that Isabella gets frustrated and loses control of her temper sometimes. The specific example was a day when the family were going out and she refused to get dressed. What followed was a good example of Isabella's mother, Susan, getting hooked into Isabella's behaviour and trying to get her to stop. It didn't work and it ended up with Susan losing control. On page 46 we focused on Susan and how she could minimise the effect of her losing control. Let's focus on how she can help Isabella.

Susan does a good job of making sure that Isabella understands the consequences of her tantrums and the effect they have on other people. Susan and Isabella have also discussed what they want in the future – for Isabella to get dressed quickly when asked without having a tantrum.

So how come Isabella continues to have the tantrums about getting dressed?

Isabella's bad behaviour continues because Susan doesn't have the crucial missing piece of Isabella's internal strategy for getting into a state like that. Susan doesn't know what *causes* the tantrums.

So although Susan is sure about what she wants – Isabella to stop having tantrums and get dressed nicely – she doesn't know what Isabella needs in order to make her stop. Once she knows what causes Isabella's frustration, they can agree on the course of action.

Here's what happened when she asked questions:

Susan: *What caused you to lose your temper in the first place?*

Isabella: *I looked in my drawer and I didn't know what clothes to choose.*

Susan: *So you didn't know what clothes to choose?*

Isabella: *No.*

Susan: *How did you know that you didn't know what clothes to choose?*

Isabella: *I don't know, I just didn't.*

Susan: *Were you making any pictures?*

Isabella: *No – nothing.*

Susan: *So your mind was blank?*

Isabella: *Yes.*

Susan: *And then what happened?*

Isabella: *[getting frustrated] I don't know – I didn't know what to choose.*

What can we deduce from this exchange?

What Susan found out was that Isabella seeing her clothes is the trigger that makes her realise that she needs to make a decision and when Isabella knows she needs to make a decision, *she draws a blank*. She doesn't have an effective decision-making strategy. She literally has a blank space in her mind where a decision-making strategy should be. This makes her frustrated, and the more she is put under pressure, the more frustrated she gets.

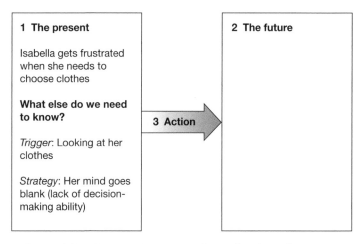

So what would be the agreed outcome to fit into 'the future'? What does Isabella need that would mean that she would not get frustrated and not have a tantrum?

Isabella needs a decision-making strategy. If she had one, it would interrupt her strategy for having a tantrum.

This is how they agreed the outcome:

Susan: *You don't want to carry on having tantrums do you?*

Isabella: *No.*

Notice that Susan's statement is phrased in terms of what Isabella doesn't want, so she needs to rephrase it.

Susan: *So let's think about what it would be like if you behaved well when I asked you to get dressed. Can you get a picture of you making a choice easily and putting the clothes on?*

Isabella: *Yes.*

Susan: *So what would that be like if you did that?*

Isabella: *Fine.*

Susan has asked Isabella to mentally rehearse the outcome. And next she can ask her to think through the consequences.

Susan: *And what would happen next if you got dressed nicely in that way?*

Isabella: *You wouldn't be cross with me.*

What do you notice about Isabella's answer here? What is her internal representation of the consequences?

It is of Susan being cross. If Susan wants Isabella to feel compelled to change her behaviour, Isabella needs positive consequences, too.

Susan: *So if I 'wouldn't be cross with you', what would I be instead?*

Isabella: *You would be pleased with me.*

That's a more useful internal representation. Susan can take this one step further to get Isabella more connected to the statement 'You would be pleased with me.' Here's how:

Susan: *And what's it like for you when I'm pleased with you?*

Isabella: *I like it.*

Susan: *And what else happens?*

Isabella: *We have a good time together.*

Susan spent some time making 'the future' compelling for Isabella.

Going through this process helps Isabella to feel motivated to change her behaviour because she has rehearsed the positive consequences of behaving well. So now all that remains is for Susan and Isabella to agree to the action, which is to learn how to make simple decisions.

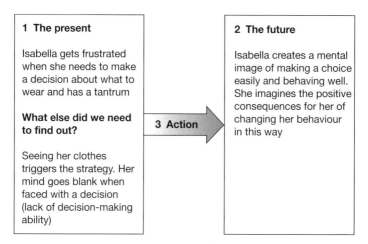

Action

Susan and Isabella decided to learn some good ways to make decisions. They agreed to make it a project for Isabella to find out how her friends made decisions, to see if she could adopt their strategies.

What did making it a project do for Isabella? It gave her responsibility for changing her behaviour and learning something new. It also meant that she needed to go and ask her friends some questions about their strategies, which taught her about being interested in other people's internal processes. As a by-product she learned about how to learn, even though she would not have any conscious awareness of that. Some pretty amazing side effects!

brilliant example

Tara's story

We are lucky enough to go on holiday with some great friends of ours most summers. At the time of this particular holiday, their three daughters, Ella, Tara and Martha, were six, five and two years old respectively. The girls and our two children are all great friends so it was very exciting for us all.

One of the most exciting things for all the children was being able to swim every day in the villa's swimming pool. This was the first year that the four older children were fairly confident in the water. This meant that they could spend what seemed like hours every day in the water having a wonderful time. They enjoyed jumping in and inventing elaborate games that got more daring by the day. All of them made fantastic progress in confidence and in their ability to swim. They particularly enjoyed jumping in off the side and pretending to be mermaids and dolphins.

We had one sticking point. Tara, just five, would not jump in and would not take her arm bands off, despite having made good progress in swimming lessons without them. She was getting more and more frustrated as she watched the other three jumping in and having such a great time. Her mother, Claire, and I could see how it was upsetting her and the other three children really wanted her to join in.

Claire was exasperated that no amount of coaxing and offers of help were working, and she was concerned that Tara was missing out on the fun that her friends were having.

I wondered if there was anything I could do to help. Considering how much Tara wanted to play with the others, I realised there must be something pretty powerful going on in her mind that was stopping her from jumping in.

Tara knows me very well so, with Claire's permission, I asked Tara a few questions to find out what she was thinking. The result was absolutely amazing: after only a few questions and one suggestion Tara jumped in on her own before I even had time to get into the water to catch her!

So what were the questions? First, I asked her if she *wanted* to jump in like her friends. I was pretty certain that she did, but as I prefer not to assume, I wanted to hear it from her. She said that she really wanted to, so now my job was to find out how she was making herself so anxious.

Me: *What do you think might happen if you do jump in?*

Tara: *Well, I think I might drown.*

Tara actually had an image of herself drowning as a result of jumping in. No wonder she wouldn't do it. In fact, it is a very sensible decision not to jump in if you think you are going to drown.

Finding out what was stopping Tara from jumping was the key to finding out why encouragement and coaxing wasn't working. No amount of encouragement is going to work if you have a picture in your mind of you drowning, let's face it.

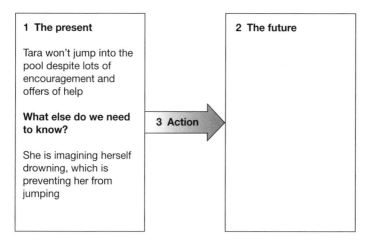

I already knew that Tara wanted to jump in because I had checked that she had the motivation to do it at the beginning of our conversation.

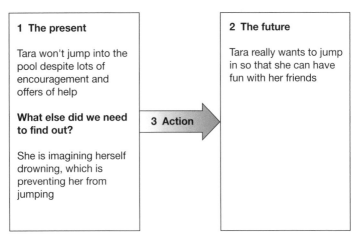

Action

Again, this was a case of the block being Tara's own imagination. To change her behaviour, I needed to help her change her thoughts.

So I asked her, 'Can you see that your friends are jumping in and *not* drowning?' Of course she could easily see that, and that question helped her to doubt her own fear.

Now was the time to help Tara to create a new image – one that was going to get rid of her anxiety and give her the courage to jump. I asked her to make a picture in her head of herself jumping in and *being safe*. The great thing about children is that they can create images instantly and without question. I suggested to her that each time she was about to jump in she could make that same picture.

I also asked her if it would help if I stood in the water to catch her. She thought that was a great idea, so I started to get in. Tara was so fast at creating the new image that when I asked her if she was ready to give it a go she just went ahead and did it, before I had time to get in! Once she had done it once, there was no stopping her. She quickly had proof that she was going to be OK and had a marvellous time with all the others.

Finally, imagine if your child comes home one day from school and says that no-one likes her. Children are very quick to make sweeping statements about themselves in this way and we need to prevent this kind of statement becoming embedded as a belief. My knee-jerk reaction to this kind of statement would be to immediately say, 'Nonsense!', partly as an emotional reaction to them even thinking that way.

brilliant tip

To find out your child's thinking behind sweeping statements, ask, 'How do you know?' or 'What do you mean by that?'

Your outcome must be to find out what your child is thinking, not to convince her that she is wrong. At this time, when she tells you that no-one likes her, she is telling you what is real for her. Once we find out her internal reality, we are in a position to encourage her to think differently.

Jennifer: *No-one likes me any more.*

Mother: *How do you know that no-one likes you any more?*

Jennifer: *Well, Mary and Elizabeth didn't include me in their game today.*

Mother: *So how does Mary and Elizabeth not including you in their game today mean that* no-one *likes you any more?*

In this example, Jennifer had attached the experience of Mary and Elizabeth not including her in their game to a meaning of no-one liking her any more.

It is in questioning this attachment that we will have the most impact. If we manage to break the relationship in her thinking between Mary and Elizabeth not playing with her and her thinking that means that no-one likes her any more, then the problem ceases to exist in its original form.

Use the Brilliant Framework as often as you can to think through problems in a logical way. Ask yourself:

● What can I ask them?

● What's happening now for my child?

● What is their strategy for getting into this problem?

● What else could they mean?

● What must be true for them to make them say what they have said?

Brilliant questions for problems

What do you mean by . . .?

This question gives you an understanding of what lies behind the surface of your child's words. It is good for clarification and avoiding assumptions.

Child: *I want to go on an adventure.*

Parent: *What do you mean by an adventure?*

What would you be doing if . . .?

This is an alternative to the above question and can be used to clarify someone's meaning too.

Child: *I just want to have some fun.*

Parent: *What would you be doing if you were having fun?*

How do you know that . . .?

We cause ourselves a lot of problems by guessing what someone else is thinking. We quite often make statements like, 'I know so-and-so will be upset if I don't tell them . . .' We think that we know the mind of the other person.

This question challenges the person to think about the evidence for their stated problem.

Child: *Sophie doesn't like me any more.*

Parent: *How do you know that Sophie doesn't like you any more?*

How is … a problem for *you*?

If we state a problem as if it doesn't belong to us, it is difficult to solve. This question reconnects the problem with the person and, as a result, the problem sometimes goes away on its own.

Child: *The girls always play on their own in the playground.*

Parent: *How is that a problem for you?*

What caused you to start feeling like this?

This is looking for the trigger for the problem. If your child is upset, it is more useful to ask what caused it than ask why they are upset.

Parent: *What caused you to get upset?*

Or,

Parent: *What happened just before you got upset?*

How did [scenario] cause you to feel like this?

This is a follow-up question to the one above, when you need more clarity.

Parent: *What caused you to get upset?*

Child: *Sally was playing with Tom at play time.*

Parent: *How did Sally playing with Tom at play time cause you to get upset?*

How does [x] mean [y]?

This question challenges the connection between one statement and another.

Parent: *What caused you to get upset?*

Child: *Sally was playing with Tom at play time.*

Parent: *How did Sally playing with Tom at play time cause you to get upset?*

Child: *It means I'm not her friend any more.*

Parent: *How does Sally playing with Tom at play time mean you're not her friend any more?*

Keep listening and keep practising these questions. The more you practise, the easier it will become and the more you will notice.

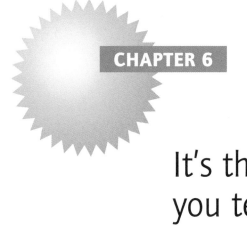

CHAPTER 6

It's the way
you tell them
– the power of
language

t is, of course, not just questions that direct our thinking, but statements too. What you say is as important as what you do. In my work as a coach, I sometimes find myself helping my clients deal with the messages they were given as children, so that they feel more positively about themselves.

In my childhood, saying that you were good at anything was considered immodest, or even boastful, and actively discouraged. It seems not very British to think, let alone say, you are good at something! It took me until I was in my thirties to say I was good at a particular thing and believe it, despite other people telling me again and again that I was. I believed that saying that I was good at something was immodest – to such an extent that I found it difficult to say it even to myself.

I want my children to develop a positive and realistic self-image. I don't believe that we should praise children for everything, because then they lose touch with reality. There is a fine line between self-confidence and self-delusion. We only have to watch reality talent shows to find examples of young people who have a distorted view of their own talents. One producer, quite rightly in my opinion, gave one mother a real talking-to for allowing her daughter to believe that she had the singing talent to win the competition, only to have her dreams and illusions shattered.

When they go out into the world, it will not help our children to think they are good at everything, just as it doesn't help children to think they are good at nothing. I want to nurture a realistic self-awareness of their strengths and encourage them to develop those strengths and interests in order to build confidence and self-esteem.

to build our children's confidence, we have to be consciously aware of the language we use

And in order to do that, to build our children's confidence and self-esteem, we have to be consciously aware of the language we use.

For example, my father used to joke that my bottom looked like two ferrets fighting in a sack! I am laughing now as I write this, and of course he thought and meant it to be funny at the time, but it's not a brilliant thing to tell a teenage girl (especially one with quite a large derrière!). Girls look to their fathers to make them feel great. It is *not* OK for you as a father to make derogatory comments to your daughter.

brilliant tip for dads

Even if you think your daughter looks awful in something, don't say it.

I am dismayed when I hear fathers criticise their daughter's appearance and then wonder why their children lack confidence.

So, in this chapter we'll take a look at how our language impacts on our children's thoughts, actions and beliefs about themselves and others. There's no doubting the importance of positive language in all aspects of communication and how easily we can instil limiting beliefs in children by the use of careless language. More specifically, we'll learn how to:

● use language that helps children to form useful beliefs about themselves and others;

- avoid 'toxic' language and make positive suggestions instead;
- use language children understand to get what you want.

What are beliefs?

Beliefs are thoughts that form our reality. They are thoughts that we consider to be true. It is now commonly accepted that 90 per cent of a child's beliefs about themselves are formed by the time they are seven. Frightening thought.

How are their beliefs formed? By a combination of experience and the example of influential people in their lives. Just think for a moment whether an adult said something to you that had a significant impact on you and changed the way you thought about something. Most of us can think of at least one example, either negative or positive. This is why, as an adult, it's so important to mind your language.

Some beliefs are positive and empowering and some are limiting in varying degrees. Your beliefs, empowering or limiting, act as filters.

What do I mean by that? What I mean is that, since beliefs are so powerful, so important to us and so much of the foundation on which we base our lives, we have a vested interest in them being *true*.

As a result, we are always looking for proof that this is so. In fact, we will, if necessary, delete or distort experiences that we have if they in any way contradict our beliefs. In other words, we filter our experiences to ensure that they fit our map of reality. Consequently, this filtering affects the way we think about the experience and also affects our behaviour during the experience.

> we filter our experiences to ensure that they fit our map of reality

Have you ever met someone who, having clearly displayed that they are good at a particular task, refuses to accept praise or recognition for it? 'Oh, it was a fluke; I'm no good at it really!' I have a friend who is absolutely sure that she is no good at maths and that it is really confusing. However, whenever we go shopping together and have to work out any calculations, she always gets the answer before me (and I was always supposed to be good at maths!). You can pretty well bet that that is a demonstration of an embedded belief that even stands the test of overwhelming contrary evidence.

And on a day-to-day basis you will hear people expressing their beliefs:

- Oh, I couldn't do that . . .
- You must never . . .
- It's always better to . . .
- People don't change.

Our beliefs remain remarkably consistent over time because we are constantly, but unconsciously, looking for evidence that they are true for us.

The *Belief Cycle* demonstrates the impact that our beliefs have on our behaviour.

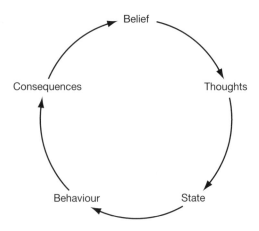

For example, I have worked with a lot of adults who believe that they are no good at speaking in front of a group of people. Here's what is likely to happen when they are asked to make a presentation.

- *Belief*: I am no good at presenting.
- *Thoughts*: Oh no. I wish someone else could do this for me. I hate it. It's going to be awful.
- *State*: Nervous, anxious and butterflies in stomach.
- *Behaviour*: If you are nervous while presenting, you are likely to avoid eye contact, speak quickly and haltingly, breathe rapidly, and display a lack of engagement with your audience and lack of confidence in your message.
- *Consequences*: The audience will be disengaged and there will be a perception of you as lacking confidence and lacking conviction in your message. As a result, your belief that you are no good at presenting will be reinforced.

The consequences of our behaviour are in line with our beliefs, proving to us that we were right to have that belief in the first place.

This is what we often refer to as a self-fulfilling prophecy. If you believe that all small business owners are out to rip you off, then every time you take your car to a garage or go to a restaurant, you'll send out all kinds of signals about not trusting the staff or the place, and you'll find that people will do the absolute minimum for you. And at worst they will even start to feel like ripping you off!

Similarly if you believe your children will never do what you ask them to, all your attention will be on thinking that they won't do what you say. And guess what . . .?

Empowering or limiting beliefs

So let's find out what some of your beliefs are, and if they are serving you well.

 **exercise**

Your beliefs

● What are your beliefs about yourself as a parent?

● What are your beliefs about your children?

● What evidence do you have to back your beliefs?

● Are your beliefs useful and empowering or do they limit you in some way?

brilliant tip

Listen out for your children's beliefs about themselves and others, so that you can help them to form beliefs that will become useful and empowering for them as adults.

Children form beliefs about themselves and others by drawing conclusions from their experiences. They attach an experience, including what is said to them, to a meaning that they create in their minds. Some of their beliefs will be empowering for them and some will be limiting or even damaging. What is lucky is that just as we are susceptible to forming limiting beliefs, we are also susceptible to positive suggestions for believing something more useful.

Our brain is a phenomenally powerful organ, which we are still only beginning to understand. It has been well documented since the 1950s that the brain records every single event in our lives. That of course includes verbal messages that we hear around us, even when we are not actively paying attention, which go straight to our unconscious mind.

Our messages to our children are a form of hypnosis. That is, language is very powerful indeed and if they hear something often enough, consciously or unconsciously, it becomes true for them.

Take, as an example, parents who talk about their children negatively within their earshot as if the child is not going to be affected unless they are talking directly to them. I'm sure most people have heard a conversation that goes like this:

Friend: *What lovely children you have!*

Mother: *Believe me, they're not usually lovely at all; they're usually really naughty.*

What messages do these children get about themselves from this exchange?

Sometimes, a child only needs to hear something once for it to become a belief.

Consider the following extreme but sadly true example.

 **example**

George's story

This happened in the 1930s to a friend of my grandfather. George was seven and an only child. He was devoted to his father and hung on his every word. They enjoyed each other's company and had a close relationship.

One day his father said to him: 'Come on George, you go up to the top of the stairs and jump and I will catch you.' George was a bit concerned, but liked jumping down the stairs, so when his father kept encouraging him and promised that he would be there at the bottom, he agreed.

▶

'Come on, George, I'm here', his Father kept saying.

George finally plucked up courage and jumped.

As he jumped, his father moved to one side and George landed in a heap at the bottom of the stairs. Confused and somewhat bruised, George looked up at his father.

'Let that be a lesson to you George: *never trust anyone.*'

Poor little George. What an extreme way to form a belief about other people. What happened to George? He grew up not trusting anyone. He was always on the lookout for people he couldn't trust and got involved with more untrustworthy people than any of his colleagues. Beliefs are self-perpetuating – we put a great deal of energy into proving to ourselves that we are right.

 **example**

Sarah's story

Sarah is 14. She came to see me because she had some difficulties at school that were a bit unusual. There were two areas that were causing the teachers and her parents concern:

● Sarah was able to solve quite complex maths problems easily, and yet consistently got easy maths problems wrong.

● Her English, which used to be excellent, had slipped in the last few years.

Let's start with the maths. She was told when she was about seven that she was no good at maths. She certainly found it difficult and formed a belief, based on her experience, that 'maths is difficult'. She had so many problems with maths that she started having extra lessons when she got to secondary school, which took her back to basics. She worked very hard on improving her maths and it all started to click into place with excellent results.

So how come she managed to solve the difficult problems now and not the simple ones? Here's how: she was so entrenched in the belief that 'maths is difficult' that when she looked at a 'difficult' problem she was OK with that – it confirmed her belief. She had caught up with her maths skills through her extra lessons and diligently worked out the problem.

However, when she looked at a problem that she considered simple, she said to herself, 'It can't be that easy.' She then thought, 'If it can't be that easy, the answer that looks obvious can't be the right answer', and she proceeded to try to get another answer, which turned out to be wrong. That's how powerful beliefs are.

I noticed a pattern in the things she was telling me. She is a very bright student – this has never been in question. However, she has been told time and time again that she 'has problems'. As a result of this, whenever she is faced, in any subject, with a simple question that has an obvious answer she finds it impossible to accept the simplicity of it and assumes that because she 'has problems' the answer has to be complex. Then she can't answer it because she has no idea what the alternative answer might be. The fact is – there is no other answer, it really is a simple question.

Believe it or not, all I had to do was to make this positive suggestion to her: 'The next time you look at something that seems easy, just say to yourself, "Great, this *is* simple!"' This suggestion made perfect sense to her. It resulted in her realisation that she had unknowingly been sabotaging her school work. Simply knowing this enabled her to stop doing it and believe that when she thinks something's simple, she's right.

There was something similar happening with her English. She had been diagnosed a few years ago with a form of dyslexia, despite not having any trouble with reading, writing or spelling. During the diagnosis she was told that she 'doesn't visualise'. She completely accepted that diagnosis from the expert, as most of us would, and as a result believed that she didn't visualise. Believe me, *everybody visualises to a certain extent.*

Believing that you don't visualise works as an instruction to your unconscious mind not pay attention to your mental images. It is essential to pay attention to those images for all sorts of activities like comprehension and creative writing.

Not paying attention to these images, even at an unconscious level, meant that Sarah's writing ability had declined. During our meeting, I noticed her visualising a lot, and pointed it out to her. She was amazed by this piece of self-awareness. I suggested that she spent some time allowing herself to day-dream and notice images as they came to mind. She was very excited at the prospect.

The power of language

All people in authority are in a position where their words can have a major impact on a young life: parents, teachers, doctors, specialists. As adults we *must* consider the potential conse-quences of the messages we give our children.

Here are some examples of statements that should carry a health warning:

- You'll never be any good at art.
- Your sister got the looks and you got the brains.
- You'll never be a singer.
- You are the class clown.
- Girls don't really need to get a good education.
- You're just like me – the black sheep of the family.
- You don't visualise.
- It's just the way you are.
- We are no good at maths in this family.

Of course, the impact of statements like these on a child largely depends on the child's personality. We have all heard stories of people who were given negative messages about themselves who then spent their lives disproving the statement and ended up being very successful.

▶ brilliant example

Opening doors

A few years ago I met someone who owned a large business. He told us that the reason he was so successful was because of a comment his headmaster had made to him when he was about 10. He had stopped to hold the door open for the headmaster and some teachers one morning. As the headmaster walked through the door, he turned to the boy and said, 'That's just about all you'll ever be good for, holding doors open for other people.' In that moment, he knew he had to prove the headmaster wrong.

That story could have had a very different ending. We cannot trust to luck that sleighting comments will turn out OK in the end.

On the other hand, my father was given the message, 'It doesn't matter how you do at school, there's a job waiting for you.' Some people might think that that was a positive message. However, it ended up having a negative impact on him because he really didn't pay any attention to how he did at school. He now wonders how his working life might have turned out if he had been encouraged to do well despite having a job lined up at the end.

Language like this contributes to children forming beliefs about themselves.

> language contributes to children forming beliefs about themselves

We must also be conscious of the 'level' at which we are addressing our children. When we are talking to our children, whether we are reinforcing good behaviour or wanting them to change what they are doing, we have choices as to the 'level' at which we address them. We can address them at the level of their identity, e.g. 'You *are* a good girl', or at the level of their behaviour, e.g. 'You behaved beautifully during the party.'

This is a very important distinction to make and we need to be acutely aware of the impact of addressing an individual at the level of their identity or belief as opposed to their behaviour.

Here are some examples of the impact of labelling children.

 **example**

Making trouble

Jonnie causes trouble in the classroom. He flicks paper clips at other desks, makes other children laugh in the class, doesn't concentrate for more than a few minutes at a time, and pulls faces at the teacher.

Consider the impact of the following statements:

- 'Jonnie, you are rude.' This is a statement of identity – who Jonnie is. This is a generalised statement that Jonnie may identify with and start to live up to.

- 'You think you can do anything you like in the class, don't you?' This is a statement at the level of belief – what Jonnie believes about his role in class. This is an extremely unhelpful statement to make for several reasons. First, it is a guess, so unlikely to be accurate. Second, Jonnie may decide that it is a good way to think and again live up to it.

- 'You are a trouble-maker.' Again, this is a statement of identity.

Labelling children in a negative way ('He's the naughty one') sticks; and human beings are fantastically good at living up to labels. The labels become self-fulfilling prophecies.

Ideas for useful things you could say to Jonnie, and indeed any children, are revealed on page 133.

brilliant example

The amber zone

Jane's young, adopted son had just started school. He was four years old.

Her son had had a challenging life until he joined his new family when he was three. He understandably had some behavioural problems. Jane worked really hard on providing him with a loving and supportive family life and on helping him to catch up on his language and social skills.

He started to get into a few scuffles with class mates in the first two weeks of school. The school had a discipline procedure which involved having different coloured zones in the classroom. If the child behaved well they sat in the green zone, then they moved to the amber zone if they behaved badly and if they persistently behaved badly they sat in the red zone.

As a result of his scuffles, he had been moved to the amber zone. Every day after the move, at least one of his class mates has said to him, 'That means you are a naughty boy.'

Let's think this through.

This process will work well with children who do not want the teacher and the other children to think badly of them. These children are likely to already have good control over their behaviour and will see the zones as a deterrent to bad behaviour and a motivation for good behaviour. These are the types of children who would probably behave well most of the time.

This process will work with older children too, for whom public disciplining and labelling is a deterrent. In fact, Jane tells me that it is so well established that some of the older children send their parents into the amber zone at home! If this is anything to go by, most older children can cope.

How useful, though, is this process for a four year old? How useful is it for this little boy to be labelled as naughty *by his peers and the school system* in his first three weeks at school?

How about the following story as an example of confusing language?

▶ brilliant example

Elizabeth's story

Alice took her niece, Elizabeth, to school on the first day of a new term. Elizabeth was seven at the time and considered very bright. The class was to be streamed into two groups for the first time and Elizabeth was in the top stream. When they arrived in the classroom, there were two large tables which had signs above them. One read 'Easy Table' and one read 'Difficult Table'.

Which one should Elizabeth sit at? The Easy Table because she finds the work easy or the Difficult Table because she will be given more difficult work than the other group?

Alice found out that, as she suspected, Elizabeth was to sit at the table labelled Difficult. What also didn't surprise her was that Elizabeth wasn't particularly pleased at having to sit there. She said that she didn't want to do difficult work because she wasn't used to finding the work difficult. She was confused because she normally finds the work easy, so why would she go to the Difficult Table? She thought she should be sitting at the Easy Table.

Even thinking about this use of language makes my brain feel like a lump of cauliflower! Not only is this labelling of the tables incredibly confusing, but what messages were the children being given and what conclusions were they going to make about their own abilities?

Children are very literal about meaning and they make meaning out of everything. They will make meaning out of confusion to make it make sense for them. What meanings will those children in that classroom make?

We can only guess, but some of them might be:

● Being clever means finding work difficult.

- Why do I find the work difficult when it says Easy Table? I must be stupid.
- Why do I have to do difficult work just because I do it quickly? I'll slow down so I can go to the Easy Table.

I'm sure that whoever put those signs up didn't *mean* to confuse anyone.

As children get older and continue to identify with the labels assigned to them, their choices become more limited. Here's what I mean: 'I can't help it; *it's just the way I am.*' As soon as someone believes that a certain way of behaving is part of their personality, they believe they can't change. I know people who were labelled bullies at school and continue to behave that way at work, well into their adult life. When they start to think of their behaviour as being *bullying behaviour* instead of being *part of their personality*, it creates possibility for change. You can change your behaviour if you want to, can't you?

How to avoid labelling

Give children negative feedback in terms of what they did – their behaviour – not what that makes them. 'Flicking your rubber at me was a silly thing to do' is very different from 'You silly boy'.

Let's return to Jonnie. Here are some behaviour-level statements that we could use:

'Jonnie, you are distracting the other children. You are making them laugh, which means they can't concentrate.'

Consider the difference in these statements:

Identity	*Behaviour*
You are a bully.	You are bullying Fred.
He's so naughty.	He behaves badly sometimes.

Giving children identity-level feedback needs to be empowering for them. 'You are kind' reinforces a kind act, for example.

Like everything else, it is important to think about the possible consequences of whatever statement you are about to make.

How to challenge your child's limiting statements

You can help your children not to form limiting beliefs by challenging statements that they make about themselves and others – statements that you consider unhelpful.

Children come out with alarmingly sweeping statements that need to be nipped in the bud:

- I'm no good at anything.
- I must be stupid if I can't do this.
- I don't like Henry any more because he doesn't get things right at school.

Knowing what you know from Chapter 6, you have the questions to challenge these.

- I'm no good at anything.
  - What do you mean you are no good at anything?
  - How does not being good at this mean that you are no good at *anything*?
- I must be stupid if I can't do this.
  - How does not being able to do *this*, make you stupid?
- I don't like Henry any more because he doesn't get things right at school.
  - How does Henry not getting things right at school cause you to decide that you don't like him any more?

The next step is to make a positive suggestion that provides them with evidence that their statement is not true.

● I'm no good at anything.

  – What do you mean you are no good at anything?

  – How does not being good at this mean that you are no good at *anything*?

  – *Positive suggestion*: Let's think of all the things you are good at. You're good at . . .

● I must be stupid if I can't do this.

  – How does not being able to do *this*, make you stupid?

  – *Positive suggestion*: You can't do this *yet* because you are learning.

● I don't like Henry any more because he doesn't get things right at school.

  – How does Henry not getting things right at school cause you to decide that you don't like him any more?

  – *Positive suggestion*: Do you think that if you didn't get something right then people wouldn't like you? Of course not. Not getting things right straight away is part of learning, and you and Henry are both learning.

How to get your children to do what you ask them!

Using positive language is an effective way to get children to understand what you want from them and to grow up as happy, confident children. It is not about simply putting a sugar coating on things.

Negatively phrased language is present all around us, even when it's well-meaning:

● Stop fighting.

● Stop shouting.

● Don't run into the road.

- Be careful you don't fall.
- Don't argue with your sister.

Remember from Chapter 2 that our minds cannot process 'not'. Negation only exists in language, not in experience.

When you tell your children, 'Don't run into the road', they have to go through a sophisticated process in order to make sense of what you said. They will immediately imagine running into the road and then have to tell themselves they mustn't do that. They still have an image of running into the road in their mind, which means they are still unconsciously paying attention to running into the road rather than staying on the pavement.

brilliant tip

We can't not think about what we don't want to think about, until we have thought about it first.

Our intention when telling our children not to run into the road is to keep them safe. A much better way to keep them safe is to tell them what we *do* want them to do: 'Stay on the pavement.' As soon as we give them an instruction like this, they imagine staying on the pavement. Running into the road doesn't even enter into their thoughts.

Putting language into positively phrased instructions – what you *do* want children to do – makes it much easier for them to comply.

The differences in the following statements are powerful. Imagine being given these instructions yourself as you read them.

Don't look at anyone else's work. Stay focused on your work.
No fighting in the playground. Play nicely with your friends.
Stop messing around. Sit down quietly.

Nobody is to run off.	Everyone stay together.
Don't forget your homework.	Remember your homework.

How many school rules are phrased in this way? Look down the list of school rules at your child's school. How many of the 'don't do this' rules could be re phrased as 'do this' instead?

How often do you hear yourself saying, 'I have just asked you not to do that, so how come you went ahead and did it?' Now you know the answer! We plant ideas in the minds of our children, unwittingly, with the use of negatively phrased language.

---

brilliant example

George's Marvellous Medicine

The children's writer Roald Dahl shows the power of negatively phrased language in the following passage from *George's Marvellous Medicine*:

'I'm going shopping in the village,' George's mother said to George on Saturday morning. 'So be a good boy and don't get up to mischief.'

This was a silly thing to say to a small boy at any time. It immediately made him wonder what sort of mischief he might get up to.

Of course it did. George had to think about mischief and make pictures of what that meant to him, in order to understand his mother's request. By the time he had flashed through some of those ideas, he was quite in the humour for making mischief!

My son came home from school last night, only to realise that he had forgotten his homework. It turned out that the last words the teacher had said to the class were 'Who thinks they will forget their homework?' Great. I bet he wasn't the only one.

brilliant tip

The key is to always think, 'What do I want the child to picture?'

My friend Fiona told me this story:

brilliant example

Fiona's story

I had three children round for tea this afternoon and an interesting 'language moment'. There were two eight-year-olds and one six-year-old. They began to play with the outside tap and the watering can. Needless to say I foresaw sodden bodies and a cross parent taking two wet children home in the car. 'Don't get wet' I said, and basically got ignored. None of them even looked up and they carried on as if I had said nothing.

I instantly realised that I had used the dreaded 'don't' word. I waited a few seconds and this time I said, 'Guys: *stay dry*', deliberately stressing the statement. Each one looked directly at me and engaged with me. They listened and they heard.

'Shall we just go and play inside?' suggested one of them, and dropped the watering can on the ground.

I couldn't believe it!

Listening to the coaching that your child's sports team gets is interesting too. Are they given instructions as to what to do in the second half of the match or what *not* to do? Are they told about what they shouldn't have done (which leaves them feeling demotivated) or are they praised for what they did well (which motivates them to do more of it).

we simply don't realise the impact of our words

We simply don't realise the impact of our words.

How many times do you hear parents say, 'I have asked her again and again not to do that and she just keeps doing it'?

My husband Tim and I catch ourselves doing this quite often:

Me: *[to Hannah on a bicycle] Hannah don't go too fast round that corner.*

[Oops! What I meant to say was: 'Hannah, slow down as you get to the corner.']

Tim: *Thomas, don't get in her way!* [Oops! 'Thomas, stand well clear.']

The difference is clear. When Thomas was given the instruction 'Don't get in her way!' he didn't move. As soon as Tim changed it to 'Thomas, stand well clear', he moved.

When we rephrase our instructions in a way that states what we want them to imagine, children comply much more easily.

I have lost count of the number of parents and teachers who tell me that knowing this and changing their language accordingly has changed their life.

It is not always easy to do either. It takes practice. We were recently with some friends whose daughter kept jumping into the swimming pool before the child in front of her had got out of the way. Her father kept saying 'Stop jumping in when Tom's still in the way – it's dangerous!' He said it again and again to no avail. We had a chat about it and he thought about phrasing his instruction differently. He was surprised at how hard he found it to think of an alternative. Finally, when he added, 'Make sure there is a clear space in front of you before you jump in', she started behaving differently.

Of course it is perfectly sensible sometimes to point out what your children should not be doing as long as you give them an instruction as to what to do instead as well.

brilliant exercise

Listen to language

Over the next week listen to your language and the language of those around you as you give instructions to your children. If you hear someone else give a negatively phrased instruction, notice what effect it has and how many times the instruction has to be repeated in order for it to have the desired effect.

If you catch yourself giving negatively phrased instructions, stop yourself and rephrase them.

How to use the power of suggestion in other places

In previous chapters I have talked about choosing our questions carefully, depending on what we want our child to think about. We have also considered the impact of asking your child (and you) to think about what you do want, not what you don't want.

The same applies to making other types of suggestions, some of which are unintentional. When we talk to someone, they have to make images in their mind to understand what we mean. And we know that what we think about has a big impact on how we feel and therefore an impact on our behaviour. As soon as we say the word 'nervous' to a child who is about to take an exam, they think about being nervous, even if you say, 'Don't be nervous' (remember our minds don't do 'not'). They are probably already nervous so it is much more useful to make a suggestion about feeling confident.

Consider the difference between how these two teachers set up a new topic:

● This next topic is really difficult. Only the cleverest ones will understand straight away.

● This next topic is something we have never done before, so it will be exciting when you all understand it.

What is the difference in your response to each of those statements?

The first teacher has created a state in the children where their focus will be on how difficult this will be and how they won't understand it.

The second teacher has created a state of interest in the children with an inbuilt assumption that they will all understand and that it will be exciting.

How much difference a few words make.

It is really useful to be able to use words carefully to suggest a positive outcome and to set your child up for a good day.

brilliant question

Before you speak to your child, first ask yourself: How do I want my child to feel after I have spoken to them?

In the next chapter we will look at how to use language to help your child learn easily and be motivated.

brilliant tips

● Think about your beliefs about yourself and your children.

● Give negative feedback in the form of statements about behaviour not identity.

- Think carefully before assigning a label to a child. Will it empower them or disempower them?

- Listen out for your child's limiting statements about themselves and others.

- Challenge limiting statements with questions, and make positive suggestions.

- Listen out for positively and negatively phrased language.

- Have a go at rephrasing negative instructions into positive instructions.

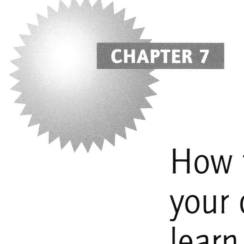

CHAPTER 7

How to help your child learn better, faster, easier

B rilliant parents understand how to encourage their children to learn, help them to get the best out of school, and allow them to continue to learn throughout their lives.

Given that we are role models whether we like it or not, *our* attitude to learning and the beliefs that *we* hold about learning will have an enormous impact on *our children's* attitude to learning and therefore their ability to learn new things.

brilliant tips

If you want to help your child get the most out of their time at school, and indeed their life, you can encourage them to think this way about learning:

- You can always learn something from any situation, however familiar.

- If someone can learn something, then you can learn it too.

- Giving something a go is more important than getting it right.

- Learn from your mistakes instead of thinking that you have failed.

- You are always capable of more.

Helping your children to learn

We, as parents, have a responsibility to support the work of our children's school through helping our children to learn at home too. We also need to notice when things aren't working as well as they could, and to be able to have constructive conversations with teachers and other people who spend a lot of time with our children.

Our children's education is a joint effort between parents and teachers, so we need to understand how learning works so that we can play an active, supporting role.

In order to learn anything effectively, your child needs to be:

● motivated to learn it;

● in a positive state when they learn it;

● able to connect the new learning to something they already know and to real life.

Keeping your children motivated to learn

Think about the last time you chose to learn something new. What was it that got you to start learning?

Were you just interested in the topic? Were you inspired by someone? What relevance did the topic have to your life? What were the positive consequences of learning it? Perhaps you just thought it would be fun.

Being motivated to learn something is vital. If a child, or an adult for that matter, is bored or demotivated in some way, they will not learn. We can support our children's motivation to learn in a few simple but important ways.

brilliant tips

- Talk to your children about what interests them.
- Be enthusiastic about their interests (even if they bore the pants off you!).
- Be enthusiastic and interested in learning – it's catching.
- Notice and reinforce the things your children respond positively to.
- Really notice what lights up their face when they talk about it.
- Encourage them to try new things.
- Make them aware of the positive consequences of learning something.

brilliant example

Ann's story

I met Ann on a workshop I was running in San Francisco. She told me this story of how she managed her daughter's negative experience with her new second grade teacher. This teacher, Mrs Johnson, is someone who teaches using negative reinforcement rather than positive. I must say that I was quite surprised by this – we are talking about California! Anyway she did.

Ann's daughter, eight, responds badly to negative reinforcement because it is important to her that the teacher likes her and likes her work. She is motivated to try harder when she is encouraged and her work appreciated.

When Ann's daughter only gets negative reinforcement, she reacts by not trying at all, because 'Nothing I do is going to make her pleased, so I'm not going to try.' As a result, she was very soon miserable about going to school.

Ann handled the situation brilliantly. She asked her daughter, 'What are the three things that are important to Mrs Johnson?'

'A tidy desk, not speaking in class without putting your hand up first and neat writing,' came the reply.

Ann asked her to just concentrate on doing those three things for a week and then they would talk about it again. Sure enough, at the end of the week, her daughter was much happier. Mrs Johnson had not needed to make any negative comments to her and in fact had given the odd hint of praise.

Ann then went to see Mrs Johnson for a parents' evening. She made no comment about her daughter's unhappiness. However, at the end of the meeting, Ann lent towards her and said, 'Just so you know, if you want my daughter to do her very best for you and go the extra mile, she responds very well to praise. She really works hard when she knows she is appreciated; just so you know,' she repeated.

Sure enough, Mrs Johnson started to write little positive comments in Ann's daughter's homework book.

Very soon, Ann's daughter became much happier and now Mrs Johnson is 'the best teacher she has ever had'!

What a fantastic intervention from Ann. There was no criticism directed towards anyone. All she did was work out how her daughter and Mrs Johnson could get the best out of each other and guide them as to how to do it. Brilliant.

---

brilliant example

Floyd's story

My husband, Tim, used to run an organisation dedicated to helping young people with significant learning difficulties to find employment. This involved teaching them the necessary social and technical skills required for a whole range of trades. Floyd was one of these young people. He was a small and slight 16-year-old who had managed to find his way through the education system without it apparently having had any impact whatsoever. He was largely illiterate and innumerate and suffered, as a result of being bullied, from an extraordinary degree of defensive behaviour, to the extent that he was hardly able to communicate verbally with anyone other than his peers.

One day, Floyd was taken ill and his supervisor, Ken, drove him home. Floyd was so grateful to him that, amazingly, he invited Ken into his house and asked if he would like to see his room. Ken could hardly help but notice that the walls were covered from floor to ceiling in posters of motorbikes, and on the floor were piles of motorcycle magazines.

At that moment Ken realised the key to Floyd's motivation. He asked Floyd to bring in his magazines, which he currently couldn't read, and designed a programme of literacy and numeracy based around motorbikes.

Six months later, Floyd could tell you the cost of the petrol required to ride a 600cc Yamaha from London to Newcastle and back – a not-inconsiderable feat of mathematical skill – and six months after that he entered his first full-time employment in the warehouse of a vehicle parts supplier.

Floyd's story is a dramatic one but the same thing happens every day in schools to a degree.

A friend of mine brilliantly got her son to read by telling him that if he wanted to build his new Warhammer tank he would have to read the instructions himself. It was a struggle for him, but because he so wanted to build it, he did it and constructed the tank all by himself. His interest in reading has increased as a result of that positive experience.

▶ brilliant example

Charlotte's story

Charlotte gets easily distracted at school. She notices everything that is happening around her – the trees blowing outside the classroom, other people talking, anything. This has a major impact on her learning and her class work.

When she started extra lessons, her teacher noted that she had no concept of the consequences of not concentrating. It had been explained to her many times but she was just not getting it. Her teacher noticed, through Charlotte's eye movements, her physiology and, through questioning, that she was talking to herself all the time. So of course she didn't hear the teacher's instructions or explanations. Her auditory channel was already full of her own conversation with herself!

Her teacher decided to show her the consequences of not concentrating, using the visual and kinaesthetic channels, thereby bypassing the auditory channel. She showed Charlotte how learning takes place through demonstrating the building of knowledge with the analogy of a brick wall. When she had put a few bricks in place, she showed Charlotte what would happen if she stopped concentrating, at that point thereby creating a gap in the brick wall. She then asked Charlotte to guess what would happen if she tried to put more bricks on top of the hole in the wall. 'Oh no – the whole wall could come down!'

Charlotte had immediately realised the impact of allowing herself to be distracted in relation to the greater consequences for her learning.

This understanding of consequences meant that Charlotte's motivation to concentrate in lessons increased dramatically.

Keeping your children in a positive state for learning

Emotional state has a huge impact on learning. Remember that state affects behaviour.

It is extremely important for children to be in a positive learning state when they are at school. Negative feelings inhibit learning, while positive feelings accelerate it. When I think back to being at school, the lessons I learnt most from were the ones that the teacher made fun, challenging and enjoyable in some way.

Children learn well when they are:

- curious
- open to new ideas
- motivated
- relaxed
- happy
- comfortable
- excited
- engaged
- challenged.

Children do not learn well when they are:

- bored
- nervous
- stressed
- anxious
- fearful
- lacking in confidence
- in an over-competitive environment
- negative.

Anxiety and fear of failure

In my work I often come across adults who do not want to ask questions in a learning environment for fear of looking stupid; I used to be like that myself. And there are many who will not answer a question unless they know they are going to get it right.

Fear of looking or sounding stupid inhibits learning.

Let's be clear; there is no such thing as a stupid question. Any question means that you are trying to make sense of something, which means that you are learning.

brilliant tip

All questions are good. Always encourage your children to ask questions.

As parents we must encourage our children to ask questions and always make them feel OK about it. If our children are going to grow up into confident adults, they must get the message that if they don't get an answer right, that's OK, they can just keep searching for the answer.

Giving it a go is more important than getting it right when we are learning. We need to challenge teachers and other adults who do not have this attitude and who make children feel bad for getting things wrong.

anxiety inhibits learning, even when a child is motivated to learn

Children learn when they feel safe and confident and when they can build on success. Children do not learn when they find a situation threatening. Anxiety inhibits learning, even when a child is motivated to learn.

I have already mentioned how we make ourselves feel anxious –

we construct thoughts of things going wrong, or otherwise failing in some way. If we are worried about failing, our attention will be on *not failing* more than it will be on achieving the task in front of us. The state of anxiety also releases chemicals into our system that inhibit our ability to think, and therefore to learn.

▶ brilliant example

Anne's story

Anne is one year away from taking her GCSEs.

She is very eloquent in class, but when she is asked to write things down in exams she just cannot get the words onto paper. She gets into a state of high anxiety and as a result can't think straight. She believes that she has something wrong with her mind that means she can't write her thoughts clearly, and this belief is in itself contributing to the anxiety.

When I elicited her strategy for getting herself into the state it was as follows:

● She already feels anxious before she goes into the exam because she believes that she will find it difficult.

● She then looks at the paper and says to herself, 'Oh my God, I have to fill that piece of paper.'

● Then she looks around and sees other people writing and starts saying over and over again, 'I must start writing.'

As a result, she cannot access any memories that she needs in order to take the exam because her thoughts are full with her talking to herself.

There is nothing wrong with Anne's mind. She simply needs to learn how to access a positive state when she takes an exam.

So how can we help our children to access positive states?

Ways to help your child get into a positive state for learning

Asking questions

Eliciting a positive state in someone is easy if you know what questions to ask and if you are in a resourceful state yourself. One friend of mine, who has started using simple techniques with her children after coming to one of our workshops, said, 'It really is just about using your brain to work out what you want and being a bit more creative in getting it.' Exactly.

The quickest way to change someone's state to a more positive one is to ask them what it is like for them to be in that positive state. The reason this question works is because in order to answer it they have to access the state first. Try it for yourself:

- What's it like when you are confident?
- What's it like when you are happy?
- What's it like when you are . . .?

You can't help feeling the emotion, can you?

So whenever you want your child to experience a particular state, ask them this question.

brilliant tip

We have found that asking 'What's it like ..?' works more effectively than other similarly worded questions such as, 'What does it *feel* like when you are confident?' They simply don't work as well, so stick to asking 'What's it like when you are . . .?'

Look up!

Notice the physiology of your child when they are in a bad mood or other negative state. It is highly likely that they will look down (see the eye movement diagram on page 168) in order to maintain the state, even if they are not aware of it. They may be talking themselves into the negative state too, which also involves downward eye movements. They may also have rounded shoulders and a generally slumped appearance.

brilliant example

Robert's story

Robert is very good at hamming up a bad mood on the way to school. Knowing what you know, you would guess correctly that he looks down at the pavement while saying to his mother, 'I really don't want to go to school, Mum. I hate school.' As his mother knows that this is a bit of an act, she can quickly move to the future state, and elicit one that is useful for Robert to go into school with. So she asks him to look up at the sky.

This, in itself, will break Robert's bad mood as he can't maintain it for long without looking down to refresh it!

When Robert looks at the sky his mother starts to ask him to make pictures about things that she knows he is looking forward to. 'Robert, can you imagine playing with your friends at break time?' 'Oh yes', he says, and immediately looks more positive and quickens his pace towards school!

brilliant example

Sam's story continued

Let's just think back to Sam the teenager. He was excellent at getting into bad moods and could even describe how he did it: 'I think of someone I don't like, talk to myself about them and look at the pavement.' After checking that he wanted to have a different experience, his father suggested he looked at the sky as he was walking along. Sam was really surprised at the difference that made to how he was feeling.

Help them to create new thoughts

In Robert's example, his mother not only got him to look up to change his state, but also asked him to create new thoughts.

brilliant tip

Creating a new internal representation can be as simple as asking your child to think of an activity that they find fun.

I quite often ask children to get a picture of themselves really having a fun time when they are in their class learning, or to make a picture of themselves concentrating well, listening well, learning easily, etc. They do it quickly and easily, it takes seconds, and it sets their focus for the day. Not only does it make it extremely likely that they will behave in the way that they have mentally rehearsed, it raises their confidence about learning. This short exercise achieves so many things – it also means that they are constantly getting a message that learning happens easily and naturally.

Storytelling, guided fantasy, metaphor and meditations

Storytelling is an excellent way of eliciting emotions in others.

Stories go straight to the most powerful part of our mind – our unconscious mind. As well as using stories to elicit states we can use them for any number of things. While we are consciously paying attention to the story, our unconscious mind is making connections and meanings at a deeper level. That means that stories are a fabulous way of helping children learn and get positive messages about themselves.

brilliant example

Stephen's story

Stephen is the deputy head teacher in a secondary school for pupils with emotional and behavioural difficulties. At the school there are a lot of young men who demonstrate aggressive behaviour; they get into fights easily and also direct their anger at themselves. Stephen is extremely dedicated to his job and has those beliefs about learning that I outlined at the beginning of this chapter. He is a great teacher – always looking for new ways to improve his own abilities and therefore improve the experience of the boys he teaches.

He came to study with us to see if he could find some new approaches to help him teach and manage the young men in his care. After the first module of the training, during which we spent some considerable time on 'state affects behaviour', Stephen went back to the school motivated to try things out. He decided that he would really concentrate on state. After the very first day back at school, he left a very excited message on our answerphone.

He told us that he had started the day with a guided relaxation fantasy. He had taken the boys on an imaginary trip to a tropical island with a cool breeze and warm sun. He took them through all the senses: what they might see (palm trees, clear blue sky, glistening turquoise sea, etc.), hear (rustling of the trees in the breeze, lapping of the waves on the shore) and feel (warm sun on their skin, sand between their toes). The boys responded very positively; they all managed a deeply relaxed state and remained a lot calmer than usual for a lot more of the day. One boy was very moved by the experience. He thanked Stephen, remarking that he had never been that relaxed in his life before.

Music

Playing upbeat music in the mornings is a great way to get everyone feeling energetic and ready for the day. Alternatively, calming music is good for those who are already a bit over-excited in the mornings!

Games and physical movement

It has long been known that learning is an active process and we learn more effectively if our whole body is involved. For some children this is crucial. At the extreme, children who have a strong kinaesthetic (feelings and action) preference for learning are sometimes labelled as slow learners or as disruptive because of their need to move around.

---

brilliant example

Hugo's story

When Hugo started his new school, he came home very excited one day, having written more than anyone else in his class about a story they were reading. His mother was surprised and delighted, as his previous school had warned her that Hugo had serious comprehension problems. The class had acted out the story so that they all experienced the emotions of the young boy in the story. Hugo was able to truly connect with the story as it came alive for him.

---

if you change your physiology, you change your state

As you know, state and physiology are linked, so it follows that if you change your physiology, you change your state. I'm sure that all of us have been in a situation where we felt that we needed to go for a walk to help us feel differently about something. And how often do our best ideas come to us when we are in the shower or bath when we are really relaxed? My best ideas come when I am on the running machine at the gym, when I reach a trance-like state – the ideas seem to come from nowhere. They don't of course; they come from my unconscious mind.

Physical activity, then, is a great way to get into a state that is useful for learning, especially if you have a child with a strong kinaesthetic preference.

Trampolines are particularly good because bouncing uses so many muscle groups, is rhythmic and encourages a connection between mind and body. If you have a trampoline, you can combine all sorts of physical and mental activities to great effect. Try doing weekly spellings or times tables with your child while they are bouncing or walking around.

brilliant example

Nancy's story

A dyslexic teacher that we know, Nicola, made the most difference to her 12-year-old pupil, Nancy, through working with her state. She noticed, in the first lesson, that when she asked Nancy to read to her, her state changed. Nicola paid attention to Nancy's physiology: shoulders going up, generally tight muscles, shallow breathing and flushed skin. In this state, Nancy's attempt to read was not particularly successful. Instead of ignoring Nancy's state, Nicola decided to work on changing it, rather than working on her reading skills. She asked Nancy to stop and asked her what happened when she asked her to read to her. Nancy replied that she immediately felt tense and panicky.

In the Brilliant Framework, this panicky state is 'the present'. Nicola knew that she needed to get Nancy into a state that would be useful for her in the future. She decided that it would really help Nancy if she could get her to feel relaxed and confident.

Nicola asked Nancy, 'What's it like when you are relaxed?' She kept asking her more questions like 'How do you know? Where do you feel it? What are you thinking about?' and kept watching for changes in Nancy's physiology.

She did the same with 'confident', once she noticed Nancy relax. Nicola made sure that Nancy was aware of the internal pictures she was making to help her feel that way, so that she could suggest to Nancy that she could think of this when she needed to be in that state.

When Nancy was in a really positive state, Nicola asked her to read to her again. Nancy could not believe the difference in her ability to read – she could see the words more clearly on the page and hear her voice more clearly.

The effect of working on Nancy's state snowballed. Reading more fluently to Nicola helped her feel more confident, and feeling more confident made her read more fluently. Soon, she surprised her teacher by agreeing to read aloud in class.

If Nicola had not known about the importance of state and behaviour, she would not have paid as much attention to it. In her opinion, she would have taken a lot longer to make progress with Nancy.

▶ brilliant example

Thomas's story

When Thomas started school, he quickly objected to doing extra reading at the end of a tiring day. Frankly, I didn't blame him; it seemed a bit much to ask a four-year-old to do homework, even if it was only for five minutes. But I began to get concerned when he consistently went into a very negative mood when I suggested reading, as he was beginning to associate reading with the bad mood. I knew that if I allowed that association to continue much longer it would affect his motivation and ability to read – potentially for the rest of his life.

Thomas was finding reading difficult and an all-round negative experience. Every time I said, 'Let's do some reading', his shoulders would slump and he would go into a very bad mood.

What I needed to do was make sure that he got into a positive emotional state when I asked him to read. So I decided to act out the story as he read. The story was one about an alien losing its socks, so it made for some hilarity as my daughter Hannah and I put our best efforts into acting it out. Thomas thought it was very funny, so we did it again the next afternoon and the next one. By the third afternoon Thomas wanted to do his reading before I asked him to. After that we didn't need to act it out either, thankfully.

His reading improved quickly because he was in a positive learning state when he started, instead of a state that blocked his learning and improvement.

brilliant exercise

Try reading a novel when you feel in a terrible mood. It is very hard to concentrate and to understand what you are reading.

State and memory

Psychologists know that information learned in a particular state will be most effectively remembered and used in the same state. If you are feeling on top of the world, that feeling will trigger memories of lots of other times when you felt that way. The same thing happens with every other emotion: sadness, joy, understanding, confusion, confidence and so on.

Therefore it is most useful to learn something in the state that you will need to recall it. Students who revise in test conditions perform better in exams than those who don't.

> it is most useful to learn something in the state that you will need to recall it

Creating the atmosphere of an exam or test, be it for SATS, music, spelling or anything else, gives our children the best possible opportunity for performing well in the test.

We learn to drive a car by driving it, not by being told how to drive it. The sooner we can put new skills to the test, in the situations where we will need them, the better.

> ### ✦ brilliant tips
>
> Get your child into a positive state for learning by:
>
> ● asking questions;
>
> ● encouraging them to look up when they are feeling down;
>
> ● helping them to create positive pictures in their minds;
>
> ● telling them stories with positive messages;
>
> ● playing upbeat (or calming) music;
>
> ● getting them to play games on the way to school;
>
> ● using the positive language in Chapter 6 to suggest having a fun day.

Helping your child to make connections for easier learning

What does connection mean? Connection means understanding. That is, our ability to make meaning from something. New information needs to be related and attached to information that we already know, in order for us to make sense of it.

Children who are good at comprehension in reading are constantly referring to their internal dictionary and making connections between that and the text. When very young children first learn to read, they have reading books that have a high ratio of pictures to words. This aids connection; that is, the word 'car' goes with a picture of a car. As readers get more competent, the amount of pictures in books decreases and the children have to make internal pictures to help them understand the story.

It's much easier to listen to a story and imagine it happening than to read it for yourself. There is an extra step when we read. We have to concentrate on reading the word and making sense of it at the same time. I am working with an adult who finds reading novels very difficult for this reason. Now he is practising reading a sentence, stopping and asking himself, 'How do I know what that means?' He is practising making full internal representations after each sentence so that he connects with the story.

So how can you help your children to make connections?

Like everything else, the first step in helping anyone is to help them become aware of their internal processes. And in order to help them become aware, you need to get really interested in how your child does what they do.

▶ brilliant example

Making connections

Here's a conversation I had with a child who is mildly dyslexic and whom I was helping with comprehension.

Me: *How do you know what the word 'table' means?*

J: *It's brown.*

I could see that she was finding a picture in her mind through looking up. I also knew that she was accessing a visual image because she said that the table was brown. Telling me that it is a certain colour presupposes a visual representation.

Me: *What's the difference between an old table and a new table?*

J: *The old one is a bit raggedy and the new one is shiny.*

Again, J was giving me visual qualities in her answers.

Me: *So you know what those words mean because you have a picture of them in your head?*

▶

J: *[looking a bit surprised] Yes, I do.*

J was now aware of her internal processes for comprehension.

I also asked her about more abstract words and we made up silly sentences for her to remember.

Then we moved on to her current spelling words for school. For each word, we did the visual spelling strategy for the actual word and attached meaning to it through deliberately creating a mental image or sentence to go alongside the word. For example:

Me: *What sort of colour would the word 'right' be?*

J: Pink.

We wrote the word out on a separate piece of paper in pink.

Me: *How do you know what 'right' means?*

J: *I don't really know.*

Me: *Well, I imagine a big tick with the word 'right' beside it.*

J: *Oh I was thinking about me with an arrow on my head pointing to the right!*

Me: *Great! It means that too.*

So for each word, we did a drawing, symbol or contextual sentence to concrete the meaning.

J was learning how she could do this for herself every time she got a new list of words. She also realised that it would be a good idea to stop and think about the words when she was reading. This would allow her time to find her internal reference for the meaning, rather than focusing so hard on the actual word that all comprehension passed her by.

J and I spent just over one hour together learning these two strategies: how to remember the spelling and how to remember the meaning. Her mother has told me that her confidence has improved tremendously. J now spends approximately a quarter of the time learning her spelling and is consistently getting most of them right, and she is choosing to read more often, which has led to a big improvement in her reading ability. Her mother told me that J volunteered to read aloud in class, which is a big step.

---

brilliant example

Hugo's story

Hugo left his school at the end of Year 3 (aged seven) to move to another part of the country. As he came out of the school gates for the last time, his teacher leant over to his mother and said quietly, 'Here are his latest test papers. I'm afraid Hugo has a quite serious comprehension problem that you might like to tell his next school about.' Hugo's mother was speechless – she had no idea, and did not appreciate hearing it for the first time in this way. She told me that Hugo didn't particularly like reading but she certainly didn't know that he had a problem.

While we were over at their house I said to Hugo, 'By the way Hugo, when you are reading, make pictures in your head as you go along so that you know what's happening.' He looked at me thoughtfully and nodded, 'OK', and ran off to find his friends.

When I next saw Hugo, his mother told me that his new school had found no evidence of comprehension problems.

Me: *Wow, Hugo, that's fantastic!'*

Hugo: *Well, Emma, you taught me how to do comprehension last time you were here.*

Me: *Did I?!*

Hugo: *Yes, you remember, you told me to make pictures when I'm reading.*

Imagine my surprise – that one suggestion had been enough to change the way Hugo understood what he was reading. Wow.

brilliant tips

brilliant tips

- Help your child's understanding by getting to know what they already know and are interested in and relate the new learning to that. Present the information in a fun way.

- Help your children understand words and prose by encouraging them to make mental images. If necessary, draw pictures for them that explain the meaning.

- Ask 'How do you know what that means?' to help them become aware of their internal dictionary.

Brilliant spelling

We now know that all excellent spellers have the same way of knowing how to spell a word, thanks to the work of Robert Dilts[1]. He interviewed expert spellers and realised that they all simply do two things:

- They see a memory of the word in their mind's eye.

- They get a feeling of familiarity if the word looks right.

brilliant exercise

Spelling

Choose a word to spell and notice how you know how to spell it. If you are a good speller, you will notice that you see the word in your mind's eye, probably above your eye line. If you are not aware of this, try spelling it backwards and you may become more aware of the appearance of the word.

If you are a less good speller, notice how you try to find the word to know how to spell it. Do you sound it out, perhaps?

[1]Adapted from *The Spelling Strategy* with kind permission of Robert Dilts.

This visual spelling strategy can be taught to just about anyone; after all, we are all able to visualise.

There is research that consistently shows this strategy to be more effective than any other strategy that is taught to our children. Thankfully, more and more forward thinking schools are teaching spelling this way.

While we were explaining the visual spelling strategy to a group of adults in one of our workshops, one of them suddenly exclaimed, 'Oh that's why I remembered some words better than others. My grandmother used to label all the pieces of furniture to help us remember what they were called and how to spell the words. I always wondered why I remember the ones that were *above my eye line* better than the others. Now I know!'

Below, I have described how to teach the spelling strategy to your child. First let me explain a bit more about eye movements and why and when it is useful to pay attention to them.

The importance of eye movements

Our eye movements unlock our thoughts. The movement of our eyes sends an electrical impulse to our brain to access certain types of sensory-based information.

- If your child is thinking in pictures, they will look up or straight out in front (as if looking into the middle distance) to see them.
- If they are thinking in sounds, describing perhaps a conversation that they had or a song that they heard, their gaze will be level – in line with their ears – either looking to the right or left.
- If they are accessing feelings or talking to themselves, they will look down.

However, you need more specific information about eye movements if you want to help your children spell effectively.

Here's a diagram of someone's eye movements, *as you look at them.* Most people's eye movements are organised this way, although a minority are organised in a way that is a mirror image of this diagram, so it is important that you check. If your child is left-handed their eye movements may be organised in the opposite way. Also, I have found that children's eye movements do not seem to settle down into regular patterns until they are about seven.

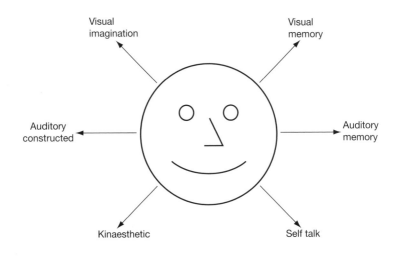

Visual
imagination

Visual
memory

Auditory
constructed

Auditory
memory

Kinaesthetic

Self talk

🔍 **brilliant** exercise

Eye movement game

To find out which side of your child's visual field is the 'memory' side, ask them these questions. The answers are not important; just the eye movements.

Visual memory

● What colour is your favourite toy?

● What was the brightest piece of clothing you wore recently?

- How many buttons has your Game Boy, TV, PlayStation, etc., got?
- What does your bedroom look like? (Ask questions about specifics in the room.)

Visual imagination

- What does a pink elephant with yellow stripes look like?
- What would a purple ice-cream look like covered in tomato ketchup?
- What would your Mum look like with green spiky hair?

Making spelling easy – the Spelling Strategy

1 Use your child's current weekly spelling list.

2 Find out where they look when accessing their visual memory (use the eye movement game to help you). For most children it will be up and to their left.

3 Explain to them that it is easiest to remember pictures when their eyes are pointed in that direction (with head facing front).

4 Ask them to think of something that they are confident and familiar with. It is very important that they are in this positive state so that when you show them the first word it will automatically become associated with 'familiarity' instead of any negative state that learning spellings might be associated with.

5 Write the first word on a plain piece of paper in a colour chosen by them. It is easier and more fun to remember things in colour.

6 Hold the word up in front of them, in their visual memory field.

7 Put the piece of paper down and replace it with a plain piece held up in their visual memory field. Ask them if they can still see the word on the plain piece of paper.

8 If the answer is 'Yes', take the plain paper away and ask them if they can still 'see' the word in their mind. If the answer is 'No' go back to step 5.

9 Ask them to spell the word backwards. They can tell you or write it down. If they write it down, make sure that they go from right to left so that the word is correctly spelt when they have finished – we don't want to create a nation of children who can only spell in reverse! The purpose of doing this is so that you can check that they really can see the word. If they cannot see it, they will not be able to do it. It is almost impossible to sound out a word backwards.

10 If they do it correctly, ask them to spell it forwards.

11 Explain to your child that when they want to remember the word again, they simply look up and to the left (or wherever their visual memory is) and see the word. If they can't remember how to spell a word, they can just look up and wait for it to appear. (It is extremely useful for younger children to be reminded during spelling tests that they should look up to find the correct spelling of the word.)

Experiment with your child. Go with your instinct and if they are finding this less easy, make suggestions: make the word more colourful, bigger or smaller, or chop the word into chunks if it is a long one. Ask them to guide you as to what helps them. Build on success.

brilliant tip

Stay curious and positive. Keep asking them what works and experiment with colours. Start with easy words.

Children are amazing. I asked one child if she could see the word in her head and to spell it backwards. She said that she could see it but that it was too far away to read. I asked her to make the word come closer. She immediately said, 'That's better, yes, I can read it now', and spelt it correctly!

I have watched mothers' jaws drop as their young son or daughter spelt a word backwards (and then forwards!) that 20 minutes earlier they had no idea how to spell. I have heard stories of children, diagnosed with severe dyslexia, having their lives changed by this simple technique of visualising words.

So, the spelling strategy is a small but significant example of how understanding internal processes, and teaching effective ones, can open up new possibilities.

> understanding internal processes can open up new possibilities

brilliant example

Naomi's story

Naomi is a 13-year-old girl who had been labelled as severely dyslexic and was very unconfident. She knew that she struggled but was desperate to be given the chance to get into the A set for the GCSE syllabus for English. Her new teacher taught her the spelling strategy and in only half an hour Naomi was able to correctly spell complex words backwards and forwards. The teacher told me that Noami was so overwhelmed at her improvement that she was almost on the ceiling with excitement! They were both in tears (of joy) at the end of the lesson, and it really has changed her life.

brilliant tips for constructive conversations

You can use everything that you have read about so far in any conversation with anyone.

For example, in a parent–teacher meeting you can:

● use the Brilliant Framework to think through what you want from the conversation

● ask questions to clarify meaning and avoid assumptions

● use positive language

● find out how you can support your child's learning at home

Summary

● Learning is an active process. The more we are asked to think about and practise what we are learning, the more effective our learning will be.

● Learning will only take place if the new information or required skill can be connected to something the learner already knows and understands. If it cannot be connected, no learning will take place.

● Children need to be in a positive state to learn effectively; anxiety inhibits learning.

● Encourage your child to ask questions by being positive about all questions. Help them to believe that all questions are useful.

● Get interested in your child's strategies for learning to make them aware of unconscious processes.

● Share your successes at home with your child's school in a positive and supportive way.

● Look for learning opportunities in everyday activities.

CHAPTER 8

Success stories

We now know that if we are going to help our child think differently, we need to understand how they are thinking and what they want.

If we don't spend time finding out how our child is creating their problem in their minds we can, at best, only guess how to help them.

If we do not spend time finding out what they want, we can only guess at solutions. I still get surprised at how easily change can happen. The more time and effort you put into finding the thinking behind the problem, the quicker the change will take place.

Putting the Brilliant Framework into action

The stories in this chapter demonstrate how we can apply the Brilliant Framework to guide our thinking in all sorts of circumstances.

Let's start by going back to Pam who I told you about on page 38 ... She got very frustrated by her nine-year-old daughter, Lucy, getting dressed slowly in the mornings and thought that it would make them late for school. As a result of realising what triggered her frustration, she was able to focus on what she wanted to happen in the mornings in order to make the changes. Here is her story in her own words.

Pam's story (continued)

Mornings in our house were a complete nightmare. I used to scream and shout at Lucy and Luke (my six-year-old) and tell them at least 25 times to do all the things that needed doing: teeth, hair, uniform, etc. Needless to say this was very tiring and left both me and the children stressed and not starting the day in the way that I wanted to. I decided to take a look at the way things worked in the house and realised it was mostly my reaction to Lucy's relaxed approach that was causing the problem – my need to be in control.

I wondered what would happen if I told them what needed to happen in the mornings and by what time and let them decide how they wanted to do it.

I sat them down and we all agreed that mornings weren't good and that things needed to change. I asked them if they were interested in trying a new way. They both agreed to give it a go so I gave them a list of all the things that needed to be done in the mornings and when they needed to be done by. I said that I would trust them to do it by themselves and that I would not remind them at all. We agreed that we would leave the house at 8.30, whatever state of dress they were in.

The following morning we started the new system. Luke was completely ready by 8.00 and had time to do some drawing and have a chat about school. I was really pleased that things seemed to be working. However, when 8.20 came and Lucy was still not dressed I had to bite my tongue. It was very hard for me not to interfere and tell her to hurry up (nearly as stressful as shouting!) as I was starting to think that she might be going to school in her pyjamas! Then a small miracle happened: she disappeared upstairs and came down, ready to leave, at 8.30.

I was very proud of them and told them so. It was a much better way to start the day and still is. I still don't understand why Lucy has to work under pressure and likes to leave things until the last minute, but I now know that it doesn't matter. I don't need to be in control of the way she works; she does it her way and I do it my way. The house is much more harmonious now that I think that way (most of the time anyway!).

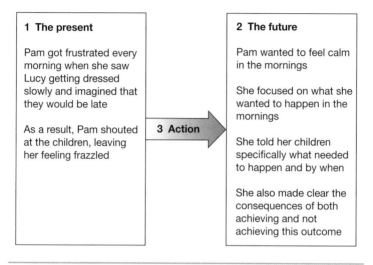

1 The present	3 Action	2 The future
Pam got frustrated every morning when she saw Lucy getting dressed slowly and imagined that they would be late As a result, Pam shouted at the children, leaving her feeling frazzled		Pam wanted to feel calm in the mornings She focused on what she wanted to happen in the mornings She told her children specifically what needed to happen and by when She also made clear the consequences of both achieving and not achieving this outcome

The key thing here was that Pam set her children an outcome: what needed to be done and by when. She then allowed her children to work out how to achieve that on their own.

? brilliant question

Are there times when you feel you need to be in control? What would happen if you allowed your children to do something in a different way?

▶ **brilliant** example

Ben and Toby's story

Ben and Toby are eight-year-old friends who play together regularly. They have a bit of a love–hate relationship. They play together well, until one of them decides they want to do something different from the activity they are currently doing. On one occasion, Ben says that he wants to play with the Lego and Toby still wants to play the Star Wars game that they have made up. Ben goes off to get the Lego out, leaving Toby in the midst of a game that he can't continue on his own.

Toby's reaction to this is to go and thump Ben. Ben turns round and thumps Toby back and a scrap ensues.

Toby's mother, Lisa, comes and tells them to play nicely, and they carry on until the next disagreement.

The boys learn nothing from Lisa's intervention and their behaviour does not change.

This is a good opportunity to use the Brilliant Framework to help the boys, particularly Toby, to think through their actions and help them develop more choices of behaviour.

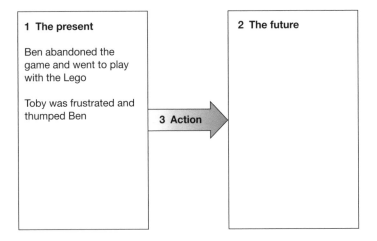

1 The present

Ben abandoned the game and went to play with the Lego

Toby was frustrated and thumped Ben

3 Action

2 The future

You can see here that Toby has not made the connection between what he wants to happen and how he goes about trying to get it!

We know what Toby wanted; he wanted Ben to carry on playing with him.

Asking him about what he wanted to happen as a result of his behaviour is much more powerful as a tool for change than assuming he has made a connection and is just badly behaved. So this is what Lisa did:

Lisa: *What did you want Ben to do?*

Toby: *I wanted him to carry on playing with me.*

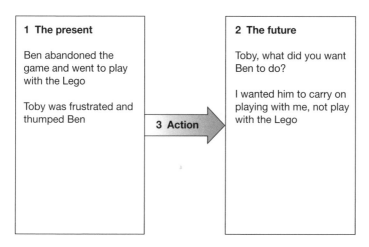

1 The present	2 The future
Ben abandoned the game and went to play with the Lego	Toby, what did you want Ben to do?
Toby was frustrated and thumped Ben	I wanted him to carry on playing with me, not play with the Lego

3 Action

Action

Now we can help Toby make the connection between his action and his intention or desired outcome. Lisa asked Toby: 'Did you think that hitting Ben would be a good way to get him to play the game with you?'

The point here was to get Toby to realise the outcome of his behaviour, which was to be told off and Ben not wanting to play, versus what he wanted.

Then Lisa asked for suggestions for ways that Toby could have persuaded Ben to go back to the game. She also included Ben, who gave Toby suggestions on how to persuade him!

What did the boys learn from this approach that they did not learn from just being told to behave? They learned to think through consequences of their actions, and to think about what they want *before* they act.

By asking Toby about what he wanted to happen, Lisa was able to relate his behaviour to his outcome.

---

brilliant example

William's story

It was the Easter holidays and we were at one of those soft-play places that are heaven for six-year-olds. There were three boys playing together who were all school friends. At one point their game became a bit boisterous, and we were wondering when one of them was either going to get hurt or come and tell on one of the others. They had long pieces of sponge and were hitting each other around the head, so it really was only a matter of time.

As predicted, one of them, William, came to say that one of the others had punched him in the stomach and the back.

My instinct was to go and deal with the perpetrator.

Instead, I followed the Brilliant Framework and asked William what he wanted me to do. He thought for a minute, smiled at us, shrugged, said 'Nothing' and ran off.

What was the difference, then, for William, between my following my instincts and following the Brilliant Framework? The key difference was that by following the framework, William was invited to consider the reason for coming to tell us. I could tell by his final smile and shrug that he had got that message. I wonder what he will do next time.

Natalie learned about the Brilliant Framework as part of a workshop I ran at her company. The same principles offer results at work as well as with children, as Natalie discovered for herself. She phoned me with her success story from home. Natalie has two sons, Constantin, 13, and Dimitri, 9. This is her story in her words.

brilliant example

Natalie's story

Last week, my eldest son came back home from school really angry and became aggressive with his brother. Dimitri was – for once (!) – innocent and hadn't provoked Constantin.

Instead of punishing Constantin for his behaviour, I decided to ask him some questions. I was able to discover that the reason for this anger was a bad mark he had in school. Practising my questions, I asked him, 'What was it about getting a bad mark in school that has caused you to feel angry?'

He replied that he was afraid of the punishment that he would get for getting a bad mark, as he had promised that morning that he had worked for his exam.

Of course I would not punish him for getting a bad mark, only for promising something that wasn't true, so I was glad to be able to clear up that misunderstanding.

My usual reaction to news of a bad mark would have been to give him a long monologue on how tired I am with telling him the same things about working in school, the importance of getting a good level in class for his future, and the fact that he is more than capable of getting good marks when he concentrates on his school books more than on his Game Boy …! Of course by repeating this once more I would have got furious with him again and sent him to his room without even listening to him or giving him a chance to talk.

▶

I knew I needed to find out more, so we calmly sat down together. I explained that I was really interested in helping him and finding out what was preventing him from preparing properly for his exams.

I went through the process of asking questions, using his words by 'bouncing from an answer to another question'.

I uncovered all sorts of valuable information: he admitted that he didn't feel comfortable with this particular teacher and that he didn't feel confident in the studying of this particular subject.

We agreed an outcome together: he wanted to feel confident in understanding this subject. I asked him to think through the consequences of understanding it and what it would be like. He seemed to be really motivated by that.

Then we planned how we would achieve that together – what help he needed from me and what he needed to do to stay focused.

He felt he was heard and respected. He even surrendered his Game Boy as a way to keep him focused during exam time. And he called me to his room the evening after to study together.

All this came from asking a few initial questions when he picked on his little brother, instead of making a judgement and sending him to his room. I feel we have made real progress.

But you're too old for tantrums!

There are some times when your child behaves *so* badly that apart from walking away and leaving them (and you) to calm down, you are at a loss as to what to do.

Here's something I have done that had a remarkable effect. I have asked the 'tantrum thrower' to write down what happened using the questions below as headings:

● What was my bad behaviour?

- What happened after I did it?
- What did I want?
- What is a better way of getting what I wanted?
- What will happen if I find a better way?
- What would be a good thing to do right now?

The act of writing about their behaviour made them consider it fully and accept that they had indeed behaved badly. They had time to think about it calmly and time to come up with some alternative ways to behave without being rushed.

brilliant example

Alice's story

Alice, 12, was taking a saxophone exam. Usually very laid back, she was very anxious about the exam. Her mother wanted to change Alice's state and do something that would make it last into the exam. She found out from Alice that the thing that was making her feel nervous (the trigger) was thinking about looking at the clock when it was her turn to go into the exam room.

She asked Alice how she wanted to feel differently. Alice said that she wanted to feel confident, so her mother asked her, 'What's it like when you are confident?'

She carried on asking 'and what's that like?' every time Alice answered the question, so that after a few times of asking Alice was very excitable and laughing. Her mother quickly said: 'Now look at the clock!'

Very cleverly, Alice's mother immediately suggested that whenever Alice looks at the clock she will feel like that. So in Alice's mind the relationship between the clock and anxiety had changed.

You may wonder if Alice was very excitable in her exam – no, she was not. What actually happened in the exam was that when Alice looked at the clock, she thought of her mother and smiled. She was relaxed.

Her mother had successfully prepared Alice to be in a different state during the exam.

▶ **brilliant** example

Hugo's story (continued)

Remember Hugo who had comprehension problems at his old school? When he got to his new school, they found no evidence of comprehension problems.

That one suggestion – to make pictures as he was reading – had been enough to change the way he understood what he was reading.

Halfway through the second term of his new school, Hugo had to take some tests. He went home and said that he knew he had done really badly.

Imagine everyone's disappointment for him when he came bottom of the class for comprehension after he had done so well in class.

His teacher was shocked and said that she really couldn't work out what had happened. Of course not – we are not taught how to ask questions to elicit strategies that don't work. We guess what has happened and try to fix what we think is the problem.

So the teacher talked to Hugo's mother about training him to take tests and putting other plans in place to solve the problem.

I had a conversation with Hugo to find out what happened:

Me: *What happened in your comprehension test, Hugo?*

Hugo: *I don't know.*

Me: *Did you make pictures of the story as you were reading?*

Hugo: *No. I didn't. You see, I like to put a lot of detail in my pictures – I like to know what the scenery is like and what the characters' faces are like ... [can you guess where this is going?!] ... and the thing is, we didn't have much time in the test so I decided not to make any pictures to save time.*

Oh my word! He decided not to understand the story to save time!

So I explained to him that it is completely necessary for him to make pictures so that he understands, but when he is in a test, he needs to put less detail into them.

His teacher doesn't need to put an action plan in place now. Hugo knows what he has to do.

brilliant tip

You can use the Brilliant Framework in any situation with anybody!

And finally ...

... a story – not mine, but nonetheless dear to me – which in some way crystallises my message to you.

Many years ago, there was a steam ship which, having been sailing the trade routes of the world for some years, had acquired a reputation for reliability. On all its voyages it had never once had any mechanical problems of any sort. Yet one day, as it was about to leave port, ready-loaded and prepared for a voyage that would take it halfway round the world, a problem of such severity developed that the engines failed and the captain was forced to abort the voyage and send for help. No-one on board could find the cause of the problem.

Residing in the port was an elderly engineer, with a reputation for being able to solve any problem that was put before him. The captain sent for him and some while later he arrived, carrying a small bag of tools. 'What's the problem?' he asked. The captain explained as best he could and the engineer asked to be taken to the engine room.

Once there, he began a minute examination of the engines; he listened and watched carefully and occasionally would call for silence so that he might concentrate even more.

After an hour he opened his tool bag and pulled out a small hammer. He walked over to a set of pipes and gave one of them a sharp tap. The engines sprang into life.

The captain stood amazed. 'Thank you, thank you,' he said. 'Tell me how much we owe you and we will pay you here and now.'

The engineer looked up. '£101' he said. '£101!' the captain exclaimed. 'You've only been here an hour and used no materials and replaced no parts. What am I paying for?'

'£1 is for my time' said the engineer, 'and £100 is for *knowing where to tap.*'

I hope this book has given you lots of ideas to help you learn where to tap with your child. There's no doubt that thinking in the way I have shown you can and will change the way you interact with and experience your children. It will change the way that they experience you. And in that new experience the seeds are sown for a future that is full of discovery and wonder.